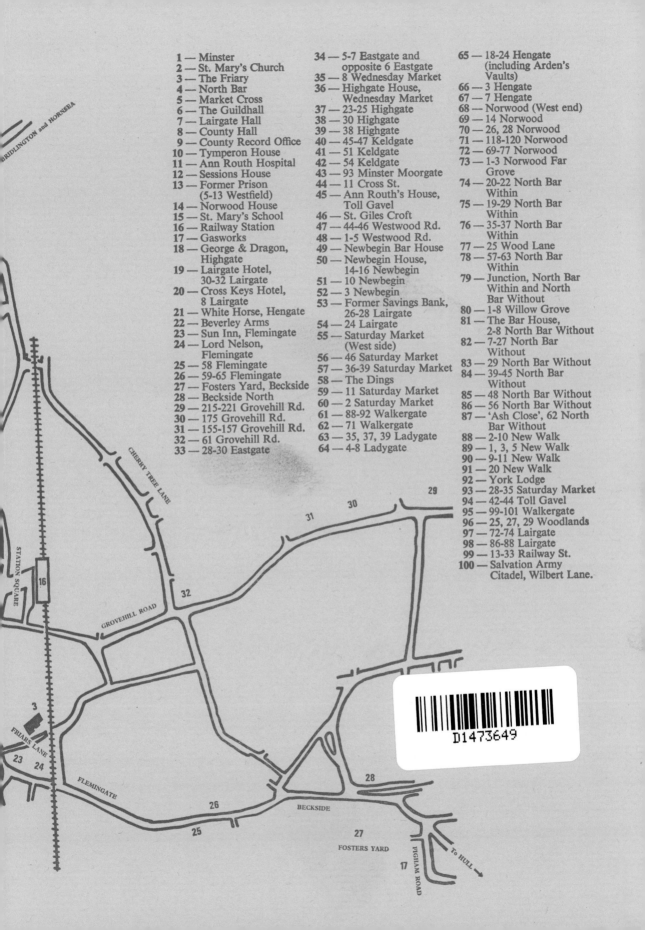

1 — Minster
2 — St. Mary's Church
3 — The Friary
4 — North Bar
5 — Market Cross
6 — The Guildhall
7 — Lairgate Hall
8 — County Hall
9 — County Record Office
10 — Tymperon House
11 — Ann Routh Hospital
12 — Sessions House
13 — Former Prison
(5-13 Westfield)
14 — Norwood House
15 — St. Mary's School
16 — Railway Station
17 — Gasworks
18 — George & Dragon, Highgate
19 — Lairgate Hotel, 30-32 Lairgate
20 — Cross Keys Hotel, 8 Lairgate
21 — White Horse, Hengate
22 — Beverley Arms
23 — Sun Inn, Flemingate
24 — Lord Nelson, Flemingate
25 — 58 Flemingate
26 — 59-65 Flemingate
27 — Fosters Yard, Beckside
28 — Beckside North
29 — 215-221 Grovehill Rd.
30 — 175 Grovehill Rd.
31 — 155-157 Grovehill Rd.
32 — 61 Grovehill Rd.
33 — 28-30 Eastgate

34 — 5-7 Eastgate and opposite 6 Eastgate
35 — 8 Wednesday Market
36 — Highgate House, Wednesday Market
37 — 23-25 Highgate
38 — 30 Highgate
39 — 38 Highgate
40 — 45-47 Keldgate
41 — 51 Keldgate
42 — 54 Keldgate
43 — 93 Minster Moorgate
44 — 11 Cross St.
45 — Ann Routh's House, Toll Gavel
46 — St. Giles Croft
47 — 44-46 Westwood Rd.
48 — 1-5 Westwood Rd.
49 — Newbegin Bar House
50 — Newbegin House, 14-16 Newbegin
51 — 10 Newbegin
52 — 3 Newbegin
53 — Former Savings Bank, 26-28 Lairgate
54 — 24 Lairgate
55 — Saturday Market (West side)
56 — 46 Saturday Market
57 — 36-39 Saturday Market
58 — The Dings
59 — 11 Saturday Market
60 — 2 Saturday Market
61 — 88-92 Walkergate
62 — 71 Walkergate
63 — 35, 37, 39 Ladygate
64 — 4-8 Ladygate

65 — 18-24 Hengate (including Arden's Vaults)
66 — 3 Hengate
67 — 7 Hengate
68 — Norwood (West end)
69 — 14 Norwood
70 — 26, 28 Norwood
71 — 118-120 Norwood
72 — 69-77 Norwood
73 — 1-3 Norwood Far Grove
74 — 20-22 North Bar Within
75 — 19-29 North Bar Within
76 — 35-37 North Bar Within
77 — 25 Wood Lane
78 — 57-63 North Bar Within
79 — Junction, North Bar Within and North Bar Without
80 — 1-8 Willow Grove
81 — The Bar House, 2-8 North Bar Without
82 — 7-27 North Bar Without
83 — 29 North Bar Without
84 — 39-45 North Bar Without
85 — 48 North Bar Without
86 — 56 North Bar Without
87 — 'Ash Close', 62 North Bar Without
88 — 2-10 New Walk
89 — 1, 3, 5 New Walk
90 — 9-11 New Walk
91 — 20 New Walk
92 — York Lodge
93 — 28-35 Saturday Market
94 — 42-44 Toll Gavel
95 — 99-101 Walkergate
96 — 25, 27, 29 Woodlands
97 — 72-74 Lairgate
98 — 86-88 Lairgate
99 — 13-33 Railway St.
100 — Salvation Army Citadel, Wilbert Lane.

Historic Beverley

HISTORIC BEVERLEY

by

Ivan & Elisabeth Hall

Documentary
Research
by
G. B. Drummond

Sponsored by:
BEVERLEY BOROUGH COUNCIL

Printed and Published by:
WILLIAM SESSIONS LTD.,
YORK, ENGLAND

Documentary
Research
by
B. A. English

This book has been published to mark the 400th Anniversary of the granting of Beverley's Charter of Incorporation by Elizabeth I in 1573.

SBN 0 900657 154 'HISTORIC BEVERLEY'
© I. & E. A. F. HALL

FOR RACHEL, JOHN AND MARGARET MIRIAM.

Printed by
William Sessions Ltd.,
The Ebor Press, York, England.
1973.

ACKNOWLEDGEMENTS

Our greatest debt is to our sponsors, Beverley Corporation, without whose generous financial help this book would not have reached publication. We are also much indebted to the Town Clerk, the Borough Surveyor and the Borough Librarian and their staff for help generously given, and to Mr. C. N. Snowden, Acting Registrar of the East Riding Land Registry, to Mr. N. Higson, East Riding County Archivist and their staff, for their assistance over a prolonged period. Dr. G. B. Drummond's thorough sifting of the 'memorials' for the Georgian period in the Land Registry, and Mrs. B. A. English's work on early maps and Victorian newspapers provided us with the vital 'key' to the mass of hitherto unexplored documentary material on property ownership in Beverley. Mrs. English also typed the manuscript. The Vicar of Beverley Minster, Rev. P. Harrison and the Minster Vergers, Mr. E. Milner and Mr. T. Edwards, the Vicar of St. Mary's, Canon S. Walker and St. Mary's Verger, Mr. R. Sygrove, have helped us on numerous occasions. Mr. D. M. Dunning, Mr. C. N. Hobson, Messrs. Robinson, Sheffield and Till, and Mr. S. Todd, have informed us of documents in their care. The late Mr. M. Burgess, Mr. H. Fairfield, Mrs. E. G. Hall, Mr. S. Hall, Mr. G. Jack, Miss Alison Kelly, Mr. W. H. Nichols, Mr. J. E. P. Parker, Mr. H. Peck, Mrs. M. Powell and Mr. B. Smith took the trouble to show us the deeds of their houses. Mr. S. Bell, Mr. G. Brown, Dr. T. Friedman, Miss M. Holmes, Mr. and Mrs. D. Neave, Miss Winifred Stephenson and Mr. R. Wilson have generously shared information with us.

A glance at the illustrations will reveal how many people have allowed us to 'invade' their houses. We hope that they will forgive us for not mentioning them individually. The quotation on page 8 is from Sir Nikolaus Pevsner's *The Buildings of England — Yorkshire: York and the East Riding* (Penguin Books, 1972).

Our thanks are also due to Messrs. Wm. Sessions Ltd., and in particular to Mr. J. B. Blackwell for piloting the work through to the press with a good humoured patience.

The following have kindly permitted us to reproduce illustrations listed below:
Society of Antiquaries (*fig.* 47), Beverley Corporation (*figs.* 46, 52, 53, 145, 272, 273, plan of Lairgate Hall, plan of 5-7 Eastgate), British Rail (Eastern Region) (*fig.* 260), East Riding County Record Office (*fig.* 271 and plan of Newbegin Bar House), Georgian Society for East Yorkshire (*fig.* 43, plan on page 73), Kingston-upon-Hull City Museums (*fig.* 89), Mr. and Mrs. D. Neave (*fig.* 165), The Pierpont Morgan Library, New York, U.S.A. (*fig.* 18), Mr. K. Reid and Mr. R. Swaine (*fig.* 72, plans of 57 North Bar Within and 100 Walkergate), Mrs. Turner (*fig.* 71), Victoria and Albert Museum (*fig.* 189), York Minster Library (*figs.* 8, 26, 42, 44).

The map on the front end papers is based upon an Ordnance Survey with the sanction of the Controller of H.M. Stationery Office.

Figs. 260, 272, 273 and plans of 5-7 Eastgate (end papers) were photographed by Mr. K. Pettinger, A.I.I.P.

Except for illustrations above all the photographs were taken by I. Hall for Messrs. Blenheim Fine Art Slides.

Historic Beverley

THIS BOOK DOES NOT PRETEND TO BE A HISTORY OF BEVERLEY, but rather an outline of its architectural development. Beverley is recognisably an 'historic town', but the term is perhaps rather vague — suggesting at once a picturesque huddle of ancient houses clustered round a medieval church — a Thaxted or a York, or towns such as Bath and Cheltenham where classic order prevails. In such towns (and their continental counterparts), the sense of history is immediate, inescapable. In others, for example Durham or Ely, the city is dominated by its cathedral. Beverley does not follow these patterns. The threads of its long history were more subtly woven and its Minster stands quietly aside, belonging as much to the fields as to the Market Place (fig. 1). In consequence the student of Beverley's architectural history must look more closely at the buildings before him, must learn to detect the minor changes that denote the slow transition from one period to the next. In Beverley architectural conservation has not only helped to give the town that now sought after sense of unity without uniformity but also illustrates its independence of its greater, more fashion-conscious neighbours.

The architecture of any town usually reflects the inter-play of several standard factors: the building materials locally available, the taste and affluence of the principal patrons, and the skills and attitudes of the architects and craftsmen, together with those chance local factors that in the long term have proved so influential.

Beverley was well supplied with building materials: timber, brick-clay, chalk (for mortar), osiers (for wattle infilling of timber-framed houses), sand and gravel. On its eastern boundary the River Hull is navigable, and provided a ready highway for building stone from the quarries near North Cave (via the Humber), and near Tadcaster (via the Wharfe and Ouse). Until the mid sixteenth century architectural patronage was dominated by the Church, for as well as the Minster there were three parish churches and the two friaries, building projects that would have employed hundreds of craftsmen for several generations. Bede noted that St. John of Beverley had built the first church here about 690. It was later destroyed by the Danes, but refounded as a collegiate church by King Athelstan (c. 895–c. 939) who is also said to have given the town its first charter. The Minster became notable as a place of sanctity and pilgrimage, and under its protection a town grew up on its northern side, over which the Church wielded substantial control until the dissolution of the College in 1547 (by order of Edward VI) when the Crown annexed the huge estates of the College.

Meanwhile the town had flourished. The burgesses had gained privileges by a charter of 1129, granted by Archbishop Thurstan, and in exchange for an annual rent they were granted important rights over the Westwood, one of the town's three pastures. (The origin of Swinemoor and Figham is unknown.) This grant of Archbishop Alexander Neville in 1380 was, as we shall see, to have far-reaching consequences. By the fourteenth century Beverley had become one of the leading English towns, and was famous for its wool trade. The Beck (fig. 81) was made navigable, bringing ships and ship-building nearer the town. Merchants travelled to the cities of Northern Europe, and Flemish immigrants settled in the town, an interchange that is reflected in the architecture of the Minster and St. Mary's, and in the use of brick for the building of the town's gatehouses or Bars (fig. 90). By 1500 however, the wool trade had declined and the town's prosperity was waning, though the parishioners of St. Mary's subscribed generously to the rebuilding of the nave and central tower of their church in the 1520's and the town remained an important local centre for craftsmanship.

FIG. 1 *View southwards from St. Mary's Church Tower. Hengate in the foreground; Ladygate to the left; North Bar Within into Lairgate to the right; Saturday Market and the Market Cross, (top centre); The Minster (top left corner). Note the different roof materials on the block of buildings at the corner of Ladygate and Hengate. The fashionable (and more expensive) slate is seen by the public while the cheaper pantiling is not. It is likely that most of the buildings between the Church and the Saturday Market are an encroachment on the original area of the Market Place.*

In 1573 Queen Elizabeth I granted the town its charter of incorporation, and six years later gave the new corporation a portion of the former Minster estates to ease the burden of the upkeep of that church. In consequence the corporation became responsible for building work at the Minster as well as on its own account.

Until the later seventeenth century secular building was in half-timber (*figs*. 87-89)–with unspectacular houses of very modest dimensions, but from the 1660's the wealthiest began to have houses built of brick (*figs*. 91-93). Thereafter, and at an increasing rate, small groups of houses were bought up and demolished and one or two new brick houses were put up in their stead (incorporating carefully salvaged material where possible) (*figs*. 3 & 4). If the churches began to lose their visual dominance, the town gained a new urban scale, particularly after c. 1750 when three-storied houses became more common (*fig*. 76). Tanners and lawyers invested their capital alongside that of the more enterprising craftsmen, though many a fashionable new front disguises the remnants of earlier work or betrays by its steep gables an innate conservatism that was to last until the close of the nineteenth century (*figs*. 3, 4, 5, 6 & 7).

Nevertheless Beverley had an 'air', for it had the town houses of the local gentry (though of course these were but secondary residences), and for their amusement the new Assembly Rooms (*fig*. 165) and a succession of theatres were opened (*fig*. 147). The same was true even of the grandest town mansions such as that of Sir Charles Hotham in Eastgate (*fig*. 116) or Norwood House in Norwood (*fig*. 165), but Hotham and the other eighteenth century Members of Parliament were also expected to be generous contributors to public architectural projects such as the great restoration of the Minster begun in 1717 and the building of the new Market Cross (*fig*. 10). From the middle of the eighteenth century onward the vogue for landscape gardening (*fig*. 151) posed a problem–how to live comfortably in town yet have a garden equal to your social position (e.g. *fig*. 160). The solution in Beverley was simple: buy up neighbouring small houses, demolish them and add their sites to your garden. Given the fact that the majority of the bigger houses lay between the line Lairgate — North Bar and the Westwood (and knowing that the Westwood could never be built upon), the well-to-do could live comfortably, and in an extended garden, without fear of being hemmed-in by uncontrollable development. The grant of 1380 referred to above has, in effect put a premium upon all those sites within easy distance of the Westwood. The Georgian houses have remained as such, and the houses of the Victorian infill have generous gardens too. (No less important, the co-existence of large and small houses in these areas has helped to maintain a sense of community that is often lacking in the 'estate' developments of the late nineteenth and twentieth centuries.)

Though Beverley flourished for most of the eighteenth century, by 1780 it became obvious that Hull had become the greater magnet for the enterprising craftsman, who could settle in the 'new town' then being built north of Queen's Dock. Similarly in the opening years of the nineteenth century — an era of 'public improvement', none of the grandiose schemes proposed for Beverley got further than paper plans, though isolated terraces of houses began to edge the fields. Only after 1870 were whole areas built over with houses of a similar design and in conformity with the Bye-laws, dwellings little different from their counterparts in Hull (*figs*. 261-263). From Hull too came the architects who transplanted discord among the older streets. First Cuthbert Brodrick, then the separate firm of Smith and Brodrick indulged in the Battle of the Styles — bringing in facades reminiscent of High Victorian Leeds (*figs*. 12 & 13) or the London of Norman Shaw (*fig*. 6). There was a brief revival of the art of wood-carving (pages 83, 98-99) followed by a period when Beverley became the focus of a group of artists in various media that centred round the Elwells, an era that came to an end when the 'multiples' began to build in the town, not only to a new scale, but with new materials. The clash between old and new is typified by the garage in Wednesday Market, and faced by such buildings, one can only presume that their architects no longer live near the buildings they design. It is no part of our plan to illustrate the equation: ugliness = good business.

Fig. 2 (opposite) *Nos. 35, 37 & 39, Ladygate looking towards Saturday Market. No. 35 has a Late Medieval timber frame. No. 37 is Early Georgian. No. 39 is Early 19th C.* Figs. 3 & 4 (left) *No. 7 Hengate, built for H. Spendlove in 1709.* Fig. 5 (top) *No. 26 (circa 1719) and No. 28 (circa 1880) Norwood.* Fig. 6 (above) *Newbegin Bar House built by Wrightson 1744-45 and 1 - 5 Westwood Rd., designed by Smith & Brodrick 1893.* Fig. 7 (below) *Nos. 1 - 8 Willow Grove, built by M. L. Whitton 1853 onwards.*

FIG. 8 (above). *Saturday Market in 1822 looking south. The houses to the left were built between 1740 & 1758. (For their present condition see* FIG. 9 (below).) *The first tall house on the right was built for Peter Dickons to the design of W. Middleton in 1777. Next door but one to its left was rebuilt in 1853, see* FIG. 234. FIG. 9 (below). *The East side of Saturday Market (The Dings) from within the Market Cross, mostly built by S. Smith, Jnr., 1755.* FIG. 10 (opposite). *Saturday Market and Old Waste. The Market Cross was designed by E. Shelton of Wakefield c.1711. The Bank building to the left was designed by W. Hawe in 1864. The building to the right is of 1803.*

THE BUILDING HISTORY OF THE MINSTER must be deduced from a study of the fabric, supplemented by the few published dates, the first of which is the fire of 1188. The programme of restoration that followed, included the heightening of the central tower and the superimposition of a spire — a process described by a contemporary as sewing a new patch into an old garment. Rebuilding recommenced, and collections were made toward the work in the early 1220's. In 1252 oaks were sent from the Sherwood Forest as a royal gift, and the High Altar was consecrated eight years later.

In 1305 the Minster Chapter pleaded for the return of its master mason Oliver de Stainefield, and work is likely to have been restarted on the nave about 1308 (*fig.* 21). It was certainly in progress from 1324-34, by which time the work had probably reached as far as the north and south doors. Yet more oaks were given in 1388, this time by Archbishop Neville, probably to help with the roofing of the nave. The construction of the west front (*fig.* 26) is undocumented, but it is likely to have taken place before 1416 when £40 was bequeathed by William de Waltham, a canon of York and Beverley, toward the building of a new east window that duplicates the great window at the west end.

John Harvey has suggested that Robert de Beverley (fl. 1253 — d. 1284) may have been connected with the building of the choir (*figs.* 14, 20) and transepts (*fig.* 16), before moving to London about 1253 when he was certainly working at Westminster Abbey (whose chief mason he became in 1260), and that a possible designer of the west front could be William Rolleston (fl. 1407-10) who lived in Walkergate. Rolleston was certainly involved in the building of the North Bar in 1409-10 (*fig.* 90).

Of the Saxon structure only the Frith Stool is known to survive, and of the Norman successor the only visible remains are the font (*fig.* 49), some chevron ornament that was re-used during the rebuilding of the north nave aisle and a waterleaf capital and some fragments of vaulting ribs re-used in the walling over the south-eastern transept. With the possible exception of the carved chevron, these Norman items are of late twelfth century date and may be from the restoration work of post 1188.

The thirteenth century building progressed as far as the first bay of the nave, and, as at Lincoln and Salisbury, included a double set of transepts, though at Beverley the main transepts have two side aisles not one (*fig.* 14). Sir Nikolaus Pevsner tells us that 'the Beverley system in its greatest purity is a system of small busy bands and large very quiet bands, *i.e.* wall arcading and triforium busy, main arcade and clerestory quiet' (*figs.* 16, 20).

The main arcades have tall narrow arches of about half the total height, each column (like those in the choirs of Lincoln and Southwell) a tight cluster of eight alternating shafts, now rounded, now bluntly pointed, some with a raised fillet to stress verticality, some left smooth. (The columns, like the rest of the building, have a variety of well preserved masons' marks that indicate that the work is original not a restoration.) The bases and capitals have typical thirteenth century mouldings, the capitals having a top band of Purbeck marble. The next zone, the triforium, has a double arcade, another Lincoln motif. The outer layer has small clustered Purbeck shafts and trefoil arches, masking plain arches supported by dwarf Purbeck columns. Between the upper and lower arches are deeply cut trefoils alternately open and closed. From below, and when the church had its

FIG. 11 (opposite). *The East side of Highgate beginning at No. 13. Mostly Early to Mid Georgian. The courtyard of No. 19 is shown in* FIG. 93.

FIG. 12 (above). *North Bar Without Nos. 39-45. No. 39 built by W. Middleton in 1769 (with a later top storey). No. 43 designed by Smith and Brodrick in 1880 for J. E. Elwell. No. 45 designed and built by J. E. Elwell in 1894.*

FIG. 13 (below). *North Bar Within. No. 35 built by W. Wrightson in 1740. No. 37 semi-detached houses designed by Cuthbert Brodrick in 1861.*

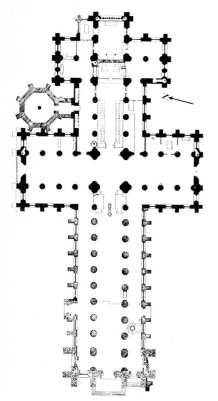

FIG. 14 (above).   *The Minster, 13th C., Greater and Lesser Transepts, S. side.*

FIG. 15 (left).   *The Minster, ground plan.*

FIG. 16 (opposite).   *The Minster, interior of Lesser Transepts from S.*

full complement of dark stained glass, the effect of this double arcading would simulate that of an open gallery of traditional form such as that of Westminster Abbey. The clerestory is about twice the height of the triforium. Two short and two tall narrow arches with more Purbeck shafts screen the plain walling on either side of the central lancet window that is framed by a much wider arch. The innermost columns are shallow fluted octagons for greater elegance (*fig.* 20). Rows of 'dog-tooth', a characteristic thirteenth century motif, decorate the arches of the second and third tiers.

The vaulting ribs spring from vaulting shafts whose capitals are level with those of the adjacent minor arches, while their lower extremities, in

the English fashion, rest on small corbels set between the main arches. On the continent, designers preferred to bring the vaulting shafts down the full inner face of the columns.

The exceptionally close spacing of the columns recalls continental rather than English usage, and when seen in perspective it is the columns not the arches that predominate, *i.e.* the solid not the space (*fig.* 21). The wall arcading is a uniform series of trefoil arches with more Purbeck shafts, and with stiff leaf capitals (*fig.* 28) of such well cut but monotonous pattern that one is tempted to believe that the master mason chose to press on with the work, rather than permit extra time to be taken up by any departure from the standard theme. This insistence on uniformity is repeated in the design of the famous chapter house staircase, whose arches are simply the wall arcading motif repeated up a double ramp, and with a minimum disturbance from the vaulting shafts of the aisle (*frontispiece*). Even the doors into the north and south transepts were given rounded tops so as not to intrude either arches or gables into the base of the principal groups of lancet windows. The southern door is subdivided by a central column (*fig.* 14), the northern one not. This use of circular forms is echoed by the rose windows in the gables, and by the much smaller inset quatrefoils that break up the wall surface over the upper tiers of windows.

Over the intersection of the choir and lesser transepts there is evidence of a change of plan. Fully worked arches and quatrefoils on one wall are partly hidden behind the present vaulting. According to Professor Willis they may represent an intended eastern gable, but in Mr. John Bilson's view they were part of an intended 'open lantern'. Furthermore, in the choir below, the spandrels over the main arches are marked out as if for ornament which, if painted, has now gone; if of carved stone diaper like that at Westminster Abbey, it was never executed.

Fig. 17 (above). *The Minster, interior of Central Tower showing Treadwheel Crane.*

Fig. 18 (left). *13th C. Illuminated Manuscript in the Pierpont Morgan Library, New York, showing a Treadwheel in use.*

Though it is likely that the Minster once had a full complement of medieval stained glass, such fragments as survived into the early eighteenth century were carefully gathered together in 1725, patterns of the leading were taken, the glass cleaned, and all set together in the east window as a part of the early Georgian restoration scheme. The rich reds and blues of the thirteenth century glass can be seen nearer the bottom of the window, the autumnal tints of the fourteenth century glass nearer the middle (beneath the stone gallery), while the fifteenth century glass occupies the remainder of the window. That in the tracery at the top is in its original position.

The most notable medieval church fittings are the sedilia (or seats for the clergy officiating at mass), the series of late fourteenth and fifteenth century carved wooden screens and the important early sixteenth century range of choir stalls (*fig.* 32). The sedilia are nicely graded in width, the easternmost and most important one being the widest. The nearby screens are of medieval date but with Georgian restoration work. The stalls date from *c.* 1520-29, and, like their counterparts at Ripon (1498) and Manchester (1508) and a set formerly at Bridlington (now scattered and depleted) are attributed to the Bromflet (or Carver) family of Ripon. The Beverley series is claimed as the largest in England, with sixty-eight stalls in a double row. The upper row has a range of canopies and canopied niches supported on oak columns which have a central knop. Originally, and as at Manchester, a horizontal carved tester completed the elaborate design. Though late in date, only some scroll work facing the north choir aisle shows any Renaissance influence. The misericords show the usual range of subjects — fabulous beasts, minor domestic comedies and tragedies (*e.g.* the fox running off with a goose, the farmer's wife in hot pursuit, etc.) jokes at the expense of the clergy (a fox preaching to geese) and armorial bearings and punning allusions to their owners' names (Wight .. weight, etc.). The Beverley set repeats at least some of the scenes found at Ripon and Manchester (*fig.* 188). The choir stalls were

much repaired by William Thornton in the eighteenth century and by James Elwell during the later Victorian period (*figs.* 33-35, 37-39).

Further east the stone reredos is largely restoration work by William Comins, the Minster master mason, of 1826, but the eastern face is original. Clustered Purbeck marble shafts support three broad arches, with elaborate niches over the columns, and between the arches and the openwork parapet, a background of richly carved diaper ornaments. As elsewhere in the church carved musicians abound. Inside the arches there is a superbly carved vault with bosses of the richest openwork foliage behind which the junction of the vaulting ribs can be seen (*fig.* 31). There is one boss showing the Coronation of the Virgin, another, a man playing a double pipe. The walls are treated as a series of blind windows with complex curvilinear tracery. As a specimen of the carvers' skill, note the man on the right hand of the northern column capital whose sleeves have each a row of the tiniest buttons. Until the Reformation the screen once supported the golden shrine of

FIG. 19. *The Minster, 14th C. Nave from S.E.*

St. John of Beverley, a shrine approached by the staircase in the turret to the east of the Percy shrine (*fig.* 22).

The latter shrine which is an acknowledged masterpiece, was erected in about the middle of the fourteenth century. It was certainly not completed before the 1330's when Edward II added the arms of France to those of England as a symbol of his claim to the throne of France. It is likely to commemorate a lady of the Percy family, though the simple tomb that (until its removal in the 1820's) lay within the arch gave no clue as to the person commemorated. Four tall slender pinnacles frame a complex gable — straight sided without, richly cusped within (*figs.* 22, 23). In between, a doubly curved arch sways upwards and outwards to support sculptured groups portraying Christ judging the soul of a lady and Christ in the act of blessing. To the left and right and upheld by crouching caryatids, angels, two holding instruments of the Passion, flank the principal figures (*fig.* 23). More angels terminate the cusps, fly upwards or downwards in the spandrels of the cusps, and sing or play musical instruments on the bosses of the vaulting. The outer and inner gables have crocketing of the greatest richness and intricacy — vineleaf and grape to the south, hazel nut to the north. The whole canopy terminates in a pair of brilliantly carved open-work foliage finials. When the shrine was new, it was luxuriously coloured and gilded. Amazingly, the shrine has suffered neither Puritanical defacement nor meddling restoration.

After the dissolution of the College in 1547 the Minster became a parish church, the octagonal chapter house of the thirteenth century, one of the earliest of its type, was demolished in 1550 and the church of St. Martin was probably allowed to fall into total ruin. The huge former Minster estates were added to those of the Crown, though a portion was later returned to the town to serve as an endowment of the fabric, but the much reduced income was insufficient for adequate maintenance and the

FIG. 22. *The Minster, The Percy Shrine, Mid.* 14th C.

structural weaknesses of the thirteenth century building became increasingly apparent — notably in the North transept where the builders, as it turned out, rashly omitted to construct the usual flying buttresses. In consequence the front of the north transept began to pull away from the remainder, until by 1716, the gable top overhung the pavement by nearly four feet (*figs*. 42, 44).

The fourteenth century master builders evidently preferred harmony to contrast (*fig*. 21), for they retained the thirteenth century internal elevations as their model, though for decorative effect they substituted carved work for Purbeck marble and for the same reasons they designed new window patterns rather than repeat the lancets of their predecessors. The tracery of the newer aisle windows is elegant and flowing, and much resembles some contemporary windows in the nave of St. Pierre at Caen in Normandy (*figs*. 186, 187). For the clerestory a much simpler tracery pattern was chosen, and continued throughout, though the adjacent vaulting followed the original quadripartite form without even the addition of a ridge rib, that was by then standard English practice (*fig*. 21). The result was certainly harmonious, but without loss of the variety beloved of fourteenth century masons. In the south aisle the wall arcading was enriched with far more carving of heads and foliage, and the arch form was 'pinched' to create an effect of inner tension (*fig*. 29). Its northern equivalent, which is somewhat later, tends to sacrifice architectural form for interesting and amusing carving (*fig*. 30). The capitals here lack boldness and the shallower, more richly carved mouldings lack the former clarity. The westernmost bays of the nave were built at the end of the fourteenth century (though those on the south side are partially eighteenth century work, for there the parish church of St. Martin abutted the south west corner of the Minster) (*fig*. 186). The new building period can be seen by the range of window tracery on the northern side and on the internal wall face over the north door, where

FIG. 23. *The Minster, The Percy Shrine, detail of carving.*

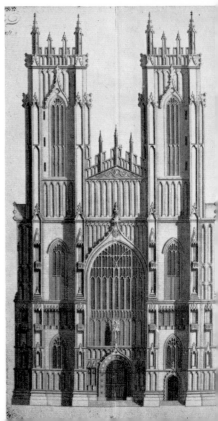

standard Perpendicular tracery was used, though only in the aisles. Perhaps the builders thought that the new north porch was a sufficient break to justify a change of window and parapet type (*fig.* 27). On the other hand the eighteenth century masons, probably one of the Issott family, ignored the Perpendicular pattern over the south door and continued the work in the Decorated style, save for the label stops of the arcading which are unmistakably Georgian.

The west front is wholly Perpendicular, and few would dispute Harvey's claim that it 'excelled almost everything previously done at the cathedrals'. It is an intricate balance of horizontal and vertical, of panelled surface and plain (*fig.* 26). The soaring buttresses suggest height (*fig.* 24) and the tympanum with its battlements and pinnacles and the deep band of panelling across the full width of the front immediately beneath it, bind the two towers together in the continental manner, so that they read as a unit, not as individual components separated by a great west window. Because the tympanum conceals the nave roof, which is much lower, it has attracted adverse criticism as a 'sham gable' (*fig.* 19), but it, and the band of panelling beneath are a later variant of the arcading of Notre Dame in Paris or the sculptured gallery at Rheims. In Paris the arcading is open, so that the peak of the roof behind is just visible, and at Rheims a gable tip crowns the three central niches. Further east in Brunswick, a double gable as at Beverley, rises high above the roof ridge. Hawksmoor greatly admired the west front and used it as a model for his twin towers at All Souls College, Oxford and for the new towers he added to the west front of Westminster Abbey. (It might be added here that in the fifteenth century, when work on the nave of the latter was re-started, Henry Yevele the master mason continued the lines of the Early English building, though as at Beverley with modified detail.)

FIG. 24 (opposite, top). *The Minster. Early 15th C. Tower, at night, looking up.*
FIG. 25 (opposite, bottom left). *The Minster from Highgate.*
FIG. 26 (opposite, bottom right). *The Minster. View of W. front after a survey by Nicholas Hawksmoor.*
FIG. 27 (right). *The Minster. 15th C. N.W. Porch from Highgate.*

The Minster, Medieval Carvings.   FIG. 28 (top left). *Early English capital, N. Transept Door.*   FIG. 29 (middle left). *Decorated capital, S. Nave aisle.*   FIG. 30 (bottom left). *Late Decorated capital, N. Nave aisle.*   FIG. 31 (top right).   *Decorated Boss, E. side of Reredos.*   FIG. 32 (above).   *Late Perpendicular poppy head, Choir stalls.*

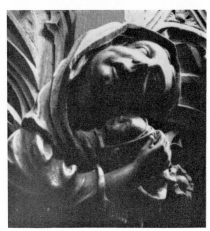

33 36 39

34 37 40

35 38 41

Early Georgian Carvings by William and Robert Thornton. FIGS. 33, 34, 35, 37, 38, 39 — *Choir Stalls.* FIGS. 36, 41 — *Great West Door.* FIG. 40 — *S. Transept Door. (Note the Thornton mixture of pagan and religious subjects, e.g.* figs. 33 and 37.)

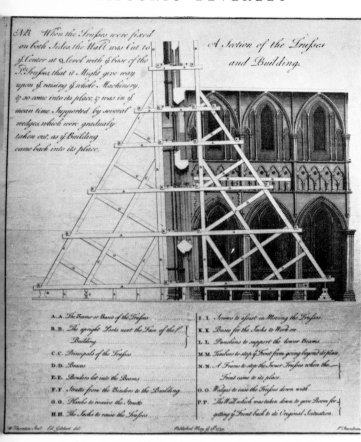

N.B. When the Trusses were fixed on both Sides the Wall was cut to ye Center at a level with ye base of the Pr Trusses, that it Might give way upon ye raising ye whole Machinery, & so come into its place. & was in ye mean time Supported by several wedges, which were gradually taken out, as ye Building came back into its place.

A Section of the Trusses and Building.

A.A. The Beams or Bases of the Trusses
B.B. The upright Posts next the Face of the Building
C.C. Principals of the Trusses
D.D. Braces
E.E. Benkins let into the Beams
F.F. Struts from the Windows to the Building
G.G. Planks to receive the Struts
H.H. The Jacks to raise the Trusses

I.I. Screws to assist in Moving the Trusses
K.K. Bases for the Jacks to Work on
L.L. Benkins to support the lower Beams
M.M. Timbers to stop ye Front from going beyond its place
N.N. A Frame to stop the Inner Trusses when the Front came to its place
O.O. Wedges to ease the Trusses down with
P.P. The Wall which was taken down to give Room for getting ye Front back to its Original Situation

FIG. 42 (opposite, top left). *The Minster. Wm. Thornton's framework used to push back the N. transept gable wall (fig. 44).*

FIG. 43 (opposite, bottom left). *Nicholas Hawksmoor's Choir Screen from an old photograph by Chas. Goulding.*

FIG. 44 (opposite, top right). *Detail of 18th C. engraving showing N. Transept and N. Hawksmoor's dome.*

FIG. 45 (opposite, bottom right). *The Minster. Present Choir Screen designed by Sir G. G. Scott and carved by James E. Elwell.*

FIG. 46 (above, left). *The Minster. Detail of drawing by T. Duncum of former Minster galleries, 1826*

FIG. 47 (left). *The Minster. Former Pulpit carved by the Thorntons.*

FIG. 48 (above, right). *The Minster. Former Nave gallery columns as re-used at 10 Newbegin.*

The church restorations undertaken during the eighteenth century have had more blame than praise. Prolonged neglect followed by bungling and parsimony, or the drastic schemes such as those of James Wyatt (dubbed 'The Destroyer'), were alike the butt of nineteenth century criticism. This gloomy picture of decay was reinforced by the collapse of the choir at Howden in 1696 and the central tower of Selby, in 1690,

and the Minster seemed destined for a similar calamity.

Nicholas Hawksmoor (1664-1736) sometime assistant to both Wren and Vanbrugh, surveyed the structure and prepared an elegantly illustrated broadsheet (*fig.* 26) to further Sir Michael Warton's and John Moyser's appeal for funds. A shower of rubble and a growing view of the sky injected urgency into the scheme, and work began in July 1717. The appeal was successful beyond expectation, and by 1730 the Minster was again in a sound state of repair, the carved woodwork restored, and new galleries, pulpit, choir-screen, altarpiece and flooring installed, mostly to Hawksmoor's designs (*figs.* 33-41, 43, 46-49, 51). He also designed the new central tower and dome in place of a much taller lantern tower (*fig.* 44).

The day-to-day responsibility was borne by the York carver-architect William Thornton (1670-1721), who devised a system of eight triangular trusses (*fig.* 42) that, in August 1719, *pushed* the transept front into position, a solution at once bold and courageous. Thornton, his son Robert (c.1703-24), his wife and her assistant John Howgill, were successively responsible for the rich Baroque 'Gothic' carving that still enriches the doors, the font cover, and the canopies of the choir stalls. Since the elder Thornton and Howgill were both paid for drawings, it seems likely that, of the woodwork, Hawksmoor designed only the galleries and the altarpiece. (While the Thorntons were carving the latter, Hawksmoor's proposals for a similar Corinthian altarpiece for York Minster were rejected, as was his scheme to put a dome on the central tower of Westminster Abbey, though his western towers for that church were clearly inspired by Beverley.)

The Thorntons' style of carving owed more to the designs of Jean Berain, than to those of Grinling Gibbons, especially the abundance of amusing small scale detail. The York carvers

FIG. 49. *The Minster. Late Norman font with Early* 18th *C. font cover by the Thorntons. The cast lead figures to the right are by Collins,* 1781. *See* FIG. 43 *for their former position.*

equally quickly absorbed the spirit of the medieval work.

The same is true of the stone carving of Thomas and John Issott of Beverley, who, alone among the masons, were paid lump sums rather than by the day. They probably did the carving of the new choir screen (*fig.* 43), and the two bays of wall arcading nearest to the font. In 1736 Thomas Issott and John Rushworth were asked to report on whether Gainsborough Parish Church should be restored or rebuilt, and for many years the Issott family were chief masons to Burton Constable.

In 1765 Thomas Lightoler designed a case for the organ built by John Snetzler. He was assisted by Thomas Atkinson (the sculptor/architect), of York (1729-98), Edmund Foster (wood carver), Giuseppe Cortese (plasterer), and William Collins (ornament modeller), another group then also at work at Burton Constable. In 1781, Collins made the statues of St. John and King Athelstan now by the south door (*figs.* 49, 181).

In all some four hundred craftsmen and labourers were employed on the restoration project, mostly between 1717 and 1731. Mr. Allanson (plumber), Joseph Burton (glazier) and Mr. Bagnall (plasterer) came over from York; the remainder were from Beverley, or exceptionally, from Hull. The most prominent names

FIG. 50 (above)   *Great West Door, 1645, at Wolfenbuttel, Nr. Brunswick, W. Germany.*
FIG. 51 (right)   *The Minster, Great West Door by the Thorntons.   Early 18th C.*

FIGS. 52 and 53. *The Minster. Water colour drawings by Hardman and Co. for windows in S. Transept.*

medieval glass and took careful tracings of the panels, then Meadley and his wife cleaned it, prior to Joseph Burton re-leading it so as to fit the east window.

The leading craftsmen employed a succession of journeymen and apprentices (some of whom served the whole of their time at the Minster). Many craftsmen also secured work for their wives and children. Mrs. Meadley, Mary Kerry and Mary Roward were stone-sawyers and general labourers, while some of their younger children cleaned bricks and did other tedious chores. Most wages were paid as day rates — 2/- — 3/- for masons, 2/- for plumbers, 1/8 for joiners as principals, and from 10d. upwards for their 'men' and their apprentices. Women usually earned 6d. a day, except when stone-sawing, for which they were paid $1\frac{1}{4}$ — $1\frac{1}{2}$d. per foot. Small children were paid 2d. — 4d. per day.

The London ironsmith who made the choir gates is not known (*frontispiece*). In 1726 John Bedell charged £12 for the pulpit wheels plus further charges from John Marshall, whitesmith, and George Best (*fig.* 47). The latter, and Thomas Robinson made the pews, the galleries and their staircases in 1722-25. These were dismantled and sold in 1826, but fragments now serve as a garden door at 10 Newbegin (*figs.* 46, 48), in the Guildhall (*fig.* 154), and in staircases at the Licensing Offices in Register Square and the Guildhall. In 1731 Thomas Gent noted that the Doric columns of the galleries were inspired by those at 'St. Albans', Rome, by which he surely meant a Roman temple at Albano near Rome. Like their medieval counterparts, many Georgian craftsmen have left their 'marks' upon the Minster.

The Georgian fittings were severely mauled during the nineteenth century. In 1826, William Comins (the resident master mason), restored the reredos, following the removal of Hawksmoor's altarpiece, and William Fowler refitted the choir when it was decided to discontinue services in the nave. From 1863-80 Sir George Gilbert Scott (1812-80) was in charge of restoration. He advised a return to the nave, designed a new choir screen (*fig.* 45), removed Fowler's galleries,

in the Minster Restoration Account Book include Edward and Thomas Robinson and George Best (carpenters and joiners), Thomas Thackera (mason), John Sanderson and Richard Meadley (bricklayers), George Burfett (stone and marble sawyer) and William Burton (plumber). The last named dismantled the

sketched out new decorations for the choir vaulting, and refitted the sanctuary (*fig.* 22). His son Oldrid designed the present choir gates in 1888. At the same time Hardman & Co. (*figs.* 52, 53) and Clayton and Bell made a series of stained glass windows, and the latter produced cartoons for the painted decoration for the vaulting over the High Altar. In 1875 Scott assured the Minster Trustees of James Elwell's competence to carve the new choir screen for the sum of £2,796. Its iron gates were the work of William Watson.

The Great Agricultural Depression seriously depleted the Minster Trustees income, though the work of repair and redecoration was continued during the time of Canon Nolloth (1880-1921). During the 1920's the increasing flow of heavy traffic past the church caused serious anxiety, and the Trustees were invited to a conference with the County Council who wished to build a by-pass.

Of the town's three medieval parish churches only St. Mary's survives. St. Martin's was once attached to the south western corner of the Minster, but it had already been demolished when Daniel King published his views of the Minster in the later seventeenth century. The former church of St. Nicholas was said to have been founded by St. John of Beverley. It had become ruinous by the mid-seventeenth century and in 1664 its parish was united with that of St. Mary. (The present St. Nicholas church was built in 1877-80, on a site north west of that of the older church.)

St. Mary's stands at the junction of Hengate and North Bar Within. Both its size and shape are masked by the narrowing of the churchyard to the north of the nave. There is more space near the north transept, but the churchyard is reduced to a mere strip at the east end. Until the end of the eighteenth century there was an even greater sense of constriction, as there were houses, not trees, to the north of the church. On the other hand the church is not at right angles to the street, and this gives the buttresses of the south transept greater prominence (*fig.* 84).

Minor fragments of Norman chancel wall can be seen serving as a foundation of the south chancel arcade, and there is re-used carved chevron round the inside arch of the south door and elsewhere. Similarly there are re-used thirteenth century carvings and mouldings in the transept arcades (*fig.* 61). The handsome windows in what is now the vestry date from c. 1280, their late Geometrical tracery the only examples of the type in Beverley. The vestry is raised above a substantial crypt which once extended further south. The choir and north east chapel are of the early fourteenth century though with a clerestorey and roof of the century following. The north and south arcades differ a little in their design, notably in the way the arches spring from the capitals, for example in the northern arcade the mouldings die away into the piers and the upper parts of the capitals are polygons rather than simple curves (*figs.* 58, 59).

The north eastern chapel is a little later. Great windows filled with rich curvilinear tracery (much like that in the nave of the Minster) occupy almost all the wall space, even the mullions are continued down the wall surface. The many ribbed tierceron vault, studded with carved bosses, seems to rise up effortlessly, an illusion in part created by the clever handling of the vaulting ribs. Between the windows

FIG. 54. *St. Mary's Church. 15th C. Misericord.*

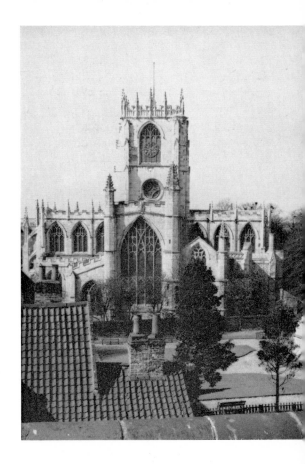

the ribs merge so as to leave only an alternation of fillet and hollow much like that of a classical column. Capitals are here restricted to the window arches. On the south side the treatment is quite different. Diminutive capitals support a few of the ribs, the rest are cunningly interwoven —a device more often employed on the continent though usually at a later date. When new, the chapel would be sumptuously furnished with stained glass windows, painted walls and ceiling (*figs. 58 and* 59).

In 1445 the panels of the wooden chancel ceiling were painted with a series of forty English Kings, *i.e.* until the reign of Henry VI. (The paintings have been twice renewed, in 1863 and 1939.)

In 1520 the central tower collapsed, ruining the nave and transepts, though the west front of c. 1400 survived and was retained in the subsequent rebuilding, as were parts of the

FIG. 55 (opposite, left) *St. Mary's W. end of Perpendicular Nave.* FIG. 56 (opposite, top right) *St. Mary's View from E. The war memorial in the foreground, designed by R. Whiteing, was modelled upon the former Wednesday Market cross.* FIG. 57 (opposite, bottom right) *St. Mary's Perpendicular S. Porch.* FIG. 58 (below) *St. Mary's Decorated N.E. Chapel.* FIG. 59 (right) *St. Mary's N.E. Chapel showing intersecting vaulting ribs.*

mid-fifteenth century transepts (*figs.* 55, 56, 57). The new work of the 1520's included new nave arcades (*fig.* 60), a new font and a splendid new central tower. The arcades resemble those of St. Margaret's Westminster (1488-1523) and those of the slightly later (*i.e.* c. 1535-45) St. Michael-le-Belfrey in York. The names of the principal donors of these new arches are inscribed upon the label stops, except on the eastern pillar of the north arcade where a group of the town's waits or minstrels is carved. The fact that at the western end there are half arches, suggests that the fate of the west front had not been finally decided when the design was submitted.

Except in the north-eastern chapel, the church has a series of fine wooden roofs of shallow pitch, one of which, until the eighteenth century, was painted with scenes from the life of St. Catherine. These ceilings, and the windows once full of stained glass, must once have presented a fine array of colour to the eye at close range. In the seventeenth and eighteenth centuries the church contained the usual array of 'box pews', galleries and monuments, almost all of which have been swept away during successive restorations, but there is one unexpected survival — the early Georgian wrought iron and marble altar, now in the south choir aisle (*fig.* 211).

The architects chiefly responsible for the successive restoration schemes were A. W. N. Pugin (the renewal of the turrets on the west front, designs for the stained glass of the west windows, the dramatic flying buttresses of the south transept, and, his last work, a sketch for a weather vane), Sir G. G. Scott (the refitting of the choir and sanctuary, including the return of the medieval choir stalls (*fig.* 54) to their former position, new altar rails, reredos, and a new nave pulpit). At the end of the century John Bilson undertook the extensive restoration of the choir screen. He also devoted many years to the critical study of the architectural development of both St. Mary's and the Minster. To these names might be added those of E. W. Pugin, Cuthbert Brodrick and Oldrid Scott.

FIG. 60 (below) *St. Mary's, View of Early* 16th C. *Nave.* FIG. 61 (opposite) *St. Mary's, View from rebuilt S. Transept into* 14th C. *Choir.*

The chief monuments in the two churches include not only the Percy Tomb in the sanctuary of the Minster, but another to the same family in the Percy Chapel (to the fourth Earl of Northumberland — a Purbeck marble tomb chest with niches that once held small figures), and two fourteenth century monuments, one with an elegant stone canopy, near the south door, another of a priest, richly robed, in the north transept (*fig.* 66). The persons commemorated are not recorded. In St. Mary's church there is a series of 'indents', i.e., the marble slabs into which engraved 'brasses' of figures, crosses and canopies were formerly inserted.

Among monuments of post-Reformation date there is a series commemorating the Warton family, the senior branch in the Minster (their chief seat was in Beverley Parks, i.e., the Minster parish), the junior branch in St. Mary's — because their house was in Newbegin. The remaining county families had estates outside Beverley, so that their monuments are usually to be found elsewhere. The earliest notable Renaissance monument is that erected by Michael Warton to his grandfather, Sir Michael Warton who had died in 1655 (*fig.* 62). The knight is shown kneeling, and in armour, within a black and white marble setting resembling an Ionic doorway. His successors' monuments in the Minster and St. Mary's have well cut marble draperies, richly framed, in the Baroque manner. Though none of them is signed, London makers seem likely (e.g. *fig.* 65).

The monument to a later Sir Michael Warton is signed by Peter Scheemakers (1691-1781), whose design is an adaptation of one by James Gibbs (best known as architect of St. Martin-in-the-Fields in London). Seated female figures (one symbolising Eternity) flank a Roman sarcophagus and urn (*fig.* 63). The only adornment of the upper part of the monument is a garland of flowers beneath the pediment. Scheemakers was the son of an Antwerp sculptor and is said to have lived in poverty in Copenhagen, before walking to Rome to complete his studies. He came to England a little before 1720, probably with Denis Plumier (1688-1721). The Warton monument presumably dates from c.1726-28, i.e., after the visit to Rome. The only contemporary monument to rival those of the Wartons is that to Sir Charles Hotham but it is of stone not marble. It was drastically cut down in 1874 at the suggestion of Sir George Gilbert Scott who disliked the great height of the obelisk. Now only the tip remains, flanked by trophies of Roman armour. (The cartouches on the title page are derived from Hotham and Pennyman monuments.)

The remaining eighteenth century monuments in the Minster are the small wall-tablets typical of their day — varying from the vigorous Baroque cartouches such as that to Mrs. Ann Routh (1722) to the elegant neo–classical figure-plus-obelisk by Peter Chenu (1760–c.1833) of London to Walter Strickland. The only outstanding late Georgian monument is that made in 1812-13 to General Bowes who died in 1812 (*fig.* 68). It is signed 'Coade and Sealy', and for it the firm charged £150 (with £26 extra for carriage charges). Coade stone or, as the firm called it, 'Lithodypra' was an 'artificial stone' of the greatest durability, and is a form of terracotta whose well guarded secret method of manufacture was neither revealed during the firm's existence nor re-discovered thereafter. The firm probably began about 1769 and continued until about 1837-40. The Coades undertook to produce first class products more cheaply than comparable work in stone or marble, and for many years they employed well known architects and sculptors as designers and modellers. In 1813 the principal modeller was Joseph Panzetta (fl.1789-1830), a pupil and assistant of Joseph Wilton who was a founder member of the Royal Academy. The inscription panel is simply framed, above which an elegant figure of Victory begins an inscription with the words 'pro patriae' (a curious error at a time when Latin was the staple of a grammar school education). Behind Victory is an urn on a 'grecian' column, to the left and right a military trophy of unexpected realism (*figs.* 68 and 69).

Church Monuments (opposite). FIG. 62 (top left) *Sir Michael Warton, d.* 1665 (*Minster*). FIG. 63 (top centre) *Sir Michael Warton, d.* 1725, *by Peter Scheemakers* (*Minster*). FIG. 64 (top right) *Detail of* FIG. 63. FIG. 65 (middle left) *Charles Warton, d.* 1714. *Detail* (*St. Mary's*). FIG. 66 (middle right) *14th C. Monument perhaps to a Percy* (*Minster*). FIG. 67 (bottom left) *William Grayburn d.* 1720 (*St. Mary's.*) FIG. 68 (bottom centre) *Maj. Gen. Bowes, d.* 1812 *by Coade and Sealy* (*Minster*). FIG. 69 (bottom right) *Detail of* FIG. 68.

There is a series of handsome black marble ledger stones in St. Mary's, with well cut inscriptions and coats of arms, but the general range of churchyard monuments is visually disappointing.

GROUND FLOOR

FIRST FLOOR

FIG. 70 (top left)   *Former Dominican Friary, 15th C. from the S.*

FIG. 71 (bottom left)   *Friars Lane Gateway, now partially demolished. 16th and 17th C.*

FIG. 72 (above)   *Plans of Friary.*

FIG. 73 (below)   *Detail of mural painting over the porch. First half 16th C.*

FIG. 74 (opposite)   *Detail of first floor room. Mid 17th C. panelling overlaying earlier wall painting.*

The surviving fragment of the Dominican Friary (founded c.1240) is one of the few such in England. Most of the Friary lay further east, i.e., beneath the present railway lines. The original function of the existing building (*fig.* 70) is a matter of conjecture, as is its architectural history, though in the opinion of Mr. K. A. MacMahon the building was the Friars' dormitory and library which was damaged by fire in 1449, and restored with substantial help from Henry VI.

The south and west walls are mostly of thin deep red brick, while the north and east fronts are chiefly of stone. Internally, however, the partition walls are timber framed, and the arrangement of the main roof trusses and their supporting posts suggests that this part of the Friary was once wholly timber framed. Probably the present facing materials: brick, stone and (internally) crude blocks of chalk date from the restorations of post 1449. The timber framework of the older partition walls is spaced so as to take an infill of thick tiles (plastered on both sides), instead of the more usual 'wattle and daub' (a technique also found in York). The existence of early Renaissance size-tempera wall-paintings on several areas of such plasterwork is clear evidence that the tile infill is not later than the earlier sixteenth century.

In plan (*fig.* 72) the Friary is an elongated L, plus a later porch. Shallow brick or stone buttresses form modest vertical accents between the very irregular rows of windows. The earliest window openings have chamfered edges, and once perhaps simply moulded brick mullions. There may have been a great bay window in the west wall. The south front is dominated by the steep gables of the west wing and the porch, their simple outlines contrasting with the Dutch gabled entrance gateways that, until a few years ago, stood in Friars Lane (*fig.* 71).

Though long subdivided into three houses, the building has much carved and moulded panelling in oak and pine. In an alcove on the first floor there were substantial remains of a mural painting with Latin inscriptions in 'black letter', and yet more in an adjacent room, over the central staircase, and in the room over the porch. The latter, in black on white, simulates a bold Renaissance damask with its medallions of double Tudor roses, fabulous beasts and melons all wreathed with interlacing ribbons (*fig.* 73). Only one Tudor fireplace survives, the remainder are eighteenth century or later. The western and central staircases are partly of winders round a newel, though the latter also had a simple mid-seventeenth century balustrade. The carved and moulded wooden panelling on the first floor is of a mid-seventeenth century date (*fig.* 74).

After the closure of Friars Lane to through traffic, the Friary and its orchard became a picturesque backwater, but since 1960, most of the site has been covered over with factory premises and the Friary subjected to neglect and vandalism. A building preservation order has been served on Messrs. Armstrong

FIG. 75 (above) *North Bar Without. The late Victorian half-timbering designed by J. E. Elwell 1892-94. The Bar House to the right refaced by W. Hawe 1866.* FIG. 76 (below) *Nos. 36—39, Saturday Market. The Bank premises were demolished in 1972. No. 37 rebuilt for the Farmar family c. 1760. No. 38, a former property of the Warton family.*

FIG. 77 (above) *Nos. 19—29 North Bar Within. No.* 21 *designed by W. Hawe*, 1886. *Nos.* 19 *and* 23, *Early Georgian. Beverley Arms Hotel largely rebuilt by W. Middleton*, 1794.

Patents Limited, the Friary's owners, and twice confirmed (in 1962 and 1965). At the time of writing, an effort is being made to secure the preservation of the building.

None of the oldest houses in the town (i.e., those built before the Restoration) have escaped serious alteration, and most lie hidden behind much later brick or plaster. There were once medieval mansions in Pighill Lane (now called Manor Road and Woodhall Way). The fragmentary foundations of one, at the northern end of Woodhall Way, were recently excavated and among the 'finds' was a substantial portion of a characteristically moulded thirteenth century multilobed column base. (In 1829 George Poulson noted that a series of tiles similar to those at Meaux abbey had been discovered in Molescroft. The Meaux tiles are also of thirteenth century date. Did they and the base come from the same building?) It is possible that the present houses 8-11 St. John Street contain substantial portions of medieval work. The older property transactions record that they were formerly the property of the College of St. John (i.e. the Minster).

Until about 1660 the typical Beverley house was of half timber and of very modest scale, often enough 'two low rooms and two garretts' beneath the thatched roof. At the back there was either a garth or garden or yet more small houses approached from the street by an arched passage beneath the 'frontstead'. Numerous such private passages still exist off the Market Places, in Toll Gavel, and in Butcher Row, though few of the houses they led to now survive. Throughout the Georgian period groups of meaner houses were bought up, demolished, and their sites built up again with one or two new brick houses. Thus in 1708 Henry Spendlove, an attorney, bought a house and three cottages and had built the present 7 Hengate as a speculation. The Tudor timbers were salvaged for re-use as roof and floor timbers. For some reason the Beverley house carpenters avoided building gables facing the main street, nor (with the known exception of 6-8 Highgate which had traceried windows), did they indulge their clients with either carving or moulding. Half timbering has been traced at 7-9, 10-12 and 49 North Bar Within, 11 (the former Lion and Lamb), 19-21 and 35 Ladygate, 18-24 Hengate, 43-44 and 55-56 Saturday Market, 6-8 and 19 Highgate, 6-7 and 15 Wednesday Market and 1 and 15 Flemingate, a modest total for what was once one of England's important medieval towns (*figs.* 80, 87-89).

The earlier houses had stout closely spaced timbers (studs). Later, house carpenters used their timber more sparingly. It was standard practice to jetty (or project) the first floor over that below with stout corner posts and curved brackets to support the overhanging storey as can still best be seen at 49 North Bar Within (*fig.* 80). (When first built this house would have looked much like the Wool Hall at Lavenham, Suffolk). In the eighteenth and nineteenth centuries the wattle and daub infill (a mixture of clay and straw rammed well into a coarsely woven mat of osiers) was either replaced by panels of plain or herring bone brickwork (*fig.* 87) or much more frequently, the timber frame was virtually concealed on the street front at least, as for example at 18-24 Hengate and 15 Flemingate. Another practice was to demolish the front portion of the house altogether, leaving the Tudor portion as servants' quarters. In such cases the panelling formerly in the reception rooms was sometimes relegated

FIG. 78 *Nos. 55—65 North Bar Within, perhaps by W. Middleton c.* 1780.

to back rooms or attics to serve as dado panelling, etc., as at 11 Wednesday Market and 7-9 North Bar Within. (Panelling from the latter is said to be that now installed in St. Mary's Manor.)

It was normal practice to leave floor joists exposed, though no doubt, as for example in Market Place Hull, the ceiling beams were either simply moulded or painted with a variety of simple designs. Fragments of painted ceiling ornament were found many years ago at 11 Wednesday Market though unfortunately their appearance does not seem to have been recorded.

Only two early window frames seem to have survived — one at the Friary, the other at 49 North Bar Within. The first has unmoulded square wooden mullions placed diamondwise, in the other example the mullions are moulded. Both have long been blocked up, hence their survival.

The familiar succession of 'styles': Baroque — Palladian — Rococo — Adam — Regency that approximately chart the course of English classical architecture from the late seventeenth to the earlier nineteenth centuries, are not so readily traceable in Beverley. In part this is because externally, at least, the houses are usually reticent, like those of Hull (but not York), in part because so many interiors have been (and still are being) gutted or 'modernised' in conformity with current fashion.

The town's architecture owes less to the architects than to the craftsmen (none of whom called themselves 'architect'), though the craftsmen had ample contact with architects when they worked upon the country houses in the vicinity. There they would see not only drawings by London and provincial architects and furniture makers, but also a wide range of architectural treatises and pattern books. For example at Burton Constable there were designs by John Carr, Thomas Atkinson, 'Capability' Brown, Thomas and Timothy Lightoler, Robert Adam, James Wyatt and Thomas Chippendale, and works as various as those of G. B. Piranesi, William Pain's *Builders Pocket Treasury* and T. Lightoler's *Gentlemen and Farmer's Architect*. By careful study of such exemplars, the more enterprising craftsman could quickly learn the latest London fashion, and adapt those elements of it as suited his or his client's need (e.g. *figs.* 118, 121). The latter included the widest range of wealth and experience. There were the local gentry (many of whom had gone on the Grand Tour), such as the Hothams and the Moysers, and some

FIG. 79 *Nos. 34—40, North Bar Within. Nos. 34 and 36 built by P. Duke 1736. No. 40 built by W. Middleton 1793-94.*

FIG. 80 (opposite)   *No. 49 North Bar Within from Tiger Lane. 15th C.*   FIG. 81 (above)   *Beckside from S. Mid and Late Georgian Houses.* FIG. 82 (below, left)   *No. 16 Hengate. The former Arden's Vaults. Early 18th C.* FIG. 83 (below, right) *Former hoist in granary above the Vaults.*

FIG. 84 (opposite) *Nos. 20 and 22 North Bar Within and St. Mary's Church from Wood Lane. Note dummy windows on top floor of No. 22.* FIG. 85 (above) *Nos. 12—24 Hengate. Nos. 18—24 Georgian refacing of half-timbered houses.* FIG. 86 (below) *Nos. 4—8 Ladygate. No. 4, Mid Georgian. Nos. 6 and 8 Victorian refacing of earlier buildings.*

of them were among the subscribers to publications such as Colen Campbell's *Vitruvius Britannicus* (*fig.* 116) (1715-25) or William Kent's *Designs of Inigo Jones* (1727) (*fig.* 118). It may be noted here that both John and James Moyser were amateur architects (*fig.* 139). In 1730 at least a dozen Beverley residents subscribed handsomely toward the cost of York Assembly Rooms, built to Lord Burlington's designs in 1731-32. About the same time, a list of principal inhabitants would have included not only Sir Francis Boynton, Sir Robert Gordon and Sir Robert Constable, but those wealthy physicians, surgeons, attorneys and apothecaries for whom many of Beverley's largest houses were built (*figs.* 128, 146, 165).

Dr. John Johnston, who bought 7 Hengate (*figs.* 3, 112) from the Constable family, is known to have gone upon a Grand Tour of Italy in 1769-71, and his contemporary Dr. John Arden was a pioneer of adult education, giving series of lectures upon 'natural philosophy' (then the usual term for science). Next came the merchants and manufacturers whose prosperity was rather more precarious, and for them houses tended to be remodelled rather than totally rebuilt, especially where the latter process could mean a temporary loss of business. The craftsmen themselves were more modestly housed, though in the fitting

Half timbered houses. FIG. 87 (below left) *No. 1 Flemingate.* FIG. 88 (above) *No. 15 Flemingate.* FIG. 89 (below right) *Nos. 6-14 Highgate, now demolished. Note 15th C. traceried window on the first floor of Nos. 4-6.*

up of their homes they occasionally used items of above average quality, which can still be found. For example there are the fine brass locks and decorated hinges in the former home of John Tygar (a whitesmith) at 46 Saturday Market (*fig.* 221). The most prosperous craftsmen—notably the Robinsons, the Wrightsons and the Middletons—owned many properties, though of course those houses they built as speculations (e.g. *fig.* 147), they were naturally anxious to sell in order to recoup their capital. One carpenter, John Ellinor, is known to have owned a slave, whom he had named 'Beverley'. The modest houses that form the bulk of the town's historic buildings, were in their day the houses of the comparatively prosperous. The poor lived for the most part in the one- or two-roomed cottages that were crowded into the narrow courts and lanes off the main streets, and these have either been demolished or converted to other uses (*see* plan on Back End Paper).

Very little has so far come to light concerning the building of private houses, though in property transactions there are occasional references to 'all that messuage or tenement lately built by' the craftsman named. Sometimes the date of a building can be deduced from the date of the mortgage that was raised to cover the cost of the new work. Fortunately the archives of the corporation are more informative, the more so as that body was also in control of the Minster and other charity estates. The selected main contractor (usually a town councillor) submitted both plan and elevation, and a written specification. The contract itself stipulated the total cost, the time allowed for construction and the dates upon which the contractor was to be paid. The contract plans and elevation survive for the Issotts' house in Butcher Row (1736) (*fig.* 271) and Anne Routh's Hospital, Keldgate (1748-50). The latter was to be built by Thomas Wrightson for £387 11s. 6d. The plan and contract (*see pages 68-69*) survive for Newbegin Bar House (*figs.* 6, 134) built by Thomas Wrightson's father William (c. 1678-1748).

FIG. 90 *North Bar from S. Built in* 1409 *at a cost of* £96. 0s. 11½d.

The easternmost portion was to incorporate an existing cottage, part of which became a sedan 'chair house' (*fig.* 135). Four years earlier the elder Wrightson had built 35 North Bar Within (*fig.* 13) on a building lease of seventy years at £5 per annum. The lease stipulated that the house 'lately built' by Samuel Smith 'now in the occupation of Thomas Hoggard' was to serve as the model. One of Smith's apprentices William Middleton (1730-1815) superseded the Wrightsons as the town's leading builder (though an isolated Minster building lease was granted to Marmaduke Constable, a carpenter, to rebuild 93 Minster Moorgate in 1758 (*figs.* 176, 184).) Middleton's work for the Minster and the Corporation includes 39 North Bar Without, 'Stanhope's House' for £345 (1769) (*fig.* 12), Newbegin Bar House, 'Mr. Dobson's house' (1779) and a series of houses in Keldgate, Minster Moorgate and on Beckside (42-44) of 1768-97, North Bar Within (*fig.* 79) and 72-74 Lairgate (*fig.* 180), as well as remodelling the Guildhall (1762-65) (*figs.* 153-7), building the Fish Shambles (1777) behind the Corn Market and Butchers' Shambles that had been built by his master Samuel Smith in 1753. These later contracts show that Middleton was responsible only for the brickwork and joinery. The plumbing, ironwork, painting and decorating was the work of others. They also show the declining use of panelling. In 1744 Wrightson had fully panelled the main rooms at Newbegin Bar House, supplying paper at 4d. and 6d. per yard only for the main bedrooms. In 1769 Thomas Dickons (a future Middleton client for the rebuilding of 57-58 Saturday Market, 1777 (*fig.* 8)) had supplied 'flower'd paper' at 2s. 6d. per piece for Stanhope's house. A decade later, Edward Elwick of Wakefield charged 3s. 6d. per piece for the 'greenstripe' paper which they put up in Mr. Dobsons' drawing room, etc. For the last house Richard Beswick grained seven doors 'Mohogane', no doubt in emulation of the fine mahogany doors at Lairgate Hall (*fig.* 170). Such documents also reveal how many important contracts were carried out by what was in effect a team of craftsmen, and how many of them frequently stepped beyond the narrow limits of their trade. The Wrightsons and Middletons between them traded in lime, brickmaking, timber, coal, iron and furniture making, as well as in land, and the leasing of tolls. John Marshall, a whitesmith, made locks for Burton Constable, the 'piece of ornament' and the chain over the font in the Minster for £6 in 1762 (*fig.* 49), and the step railings at 39 North Bar Without. Thomas Walker (fl. 1765-94) a cabinet maker, also did the finer architectural joinery, and Jeremiah (c.1726-86) and Joseph Hargrave (fl. 1766-1802) did carving in stone and wood, made furniture, and on occasion acted as architects. Only after 1770 was the traditional pattern disturbed by the introduction of ready made, sometimes synthetic, materials. Cast metals (brass, lead, iron), Coade stone (*fig.* 182), cast plaster and 'composition' all fashioned into a great variety of decorative motifs certainly saved time and labour without loss of fine finish, but ornaments that simply needed sticking or pinning into position certainly both reduced the craftsmen's scope, and made the 'local' product little different from that in Leeds, Manchester or London. It must be admitted of course that the craftsman was interested in his own survival, not that of a 'local style'. These changes reflect not only an increased demand for greater elegance, but also the increased wealth resulting from the Agricultural Revolution, and the application of new methods and materials to traditional practice was a facet of the Industrial Revolution.

Beverley's Georgian public buildings were quite modest in scale. They included the Market Cross (*fig.* 10), various almshouses (notably Tymperon's Hospital and Ann(e) Routh's Hospital) (*figs.* 138-9), the two Shambles and the Guildhall. The Cross was first suggested in 1708, but building did not begin in earnest until 1711, and payments to the workmen were still outstanding late in 1715. The building was designed, and its site chosen, by Edward Shelton of Wakefield. Eight Doric columns arranged in pairs support a Baroque dome and sharply profiled lantern, motifs perhaps derived from the lesser domes of Vanbrugh and Hawksmoor's Castle Howard, then in course of construction. The names of the craftsmen responsible are not recorded, though Edward Robinson (d.1718), a leading builder, helped to select the building materials. The eight urns, carved by Edward Rushworth, were added in 1769.

'Artisan Mannerism in brick'.   FIGS. 91 & 92 (opposite left) *No. 58 Flemingate c.* 1660-70.   FIG. 93 (opposite right) *George & Dragon yard,* 19 *Highgate, dated* 1671.

FIGS. 94-98   *No. 54* Keldgate, *built c.* 1696 *for the Constable family. The front door, and the chimneypiece in* FIG. 95 *(above right) are c.* 1770. *The overmantel painting in* FIG. 96 *(below left) is c.* 1696. FIG. 98 *(below right) shows the servants' staircase c.f.* FIG. 103, *a known work of T. Ellinor.*

The reconstruction of the Guildhall was more complex because, for economic reasons, it was decided to reface an ancient structure rather than to rebuild it. The plans of Joseph Page of Hull were rejected in favour of those of William Middleton, whose estimate amounted to £374 15s. 0d. The old front portion survived until 1832, but behind it Middleton devised a Court Room and a Jury Chamber (*see* plans, page 73). The north and south walls of the Court Room are arcaded. The west wall is dominated by Edmund Foster's richly carved frame to the Mayor's seat, and the handsome royal coat of arms above it by Guiseppe Cortese. Foster's ornamental detail closely resembles that in Chippendale's *Director*, the third edition of which was published in 1762 (*figs.* 155-6). As originally designed, Cortese's superb ceiling (*fig.* 157) would have been much simpler, but the corporation agreed to pay £25 extra for 'two large Additional Ornamental panels', whose richness Cortese complimented by 'superfluous Work done in the Cove' for which he hopefully submitted a request for another five guineas, the payment of which 'I leave Gentlemen to your discretion'. (The Doric columns (*fig.* 154) and matching balusters of the small staircase) at the east

FIGS. 99, 100 & 101 *Nos. 14-16 Newbegin built as the town house of Charles Warton c. 1680-1700.* FIG. 100 (below left) *shows the servants' staircase, the main one resembling* FIG. 97 (bottom centre opposite).

FIGS. 102, 103, 104 & 105 *No. 65 Toll Gavel. 'Ann Routh's House,' built c. 1703 by T. Ellinor. Note recessed panels at either end of facade. The number of ground floor windows was halved to save Window Tax. FIG. 105 (below) The simple Venetian window is part of the alterations c. 1730.*

end of the room once formed part of the galleries in the Minster prior to their demolition in 1826 (*fig.* 46).)

The Jury Room has an apsidal end that neatly disguises the small staircases that lead to the Court Room and the basement. Opposite, the handsome double-decker chimney piece is enriched with carving and 'fretwork'. The portrait now in the overmantel is that of William Middleton (*fig.* 153). The Guildhall was partly refurnished by William Thompson who supplied sets of arm and single chairs at 25s. and 17s. apiece (*figs.* 153, 166), a treble seated chair at £5 5s. 0d. and a pair of dining tables for which the charge was £7 10s. 0d. The chairs follow the style of those in Chippendale's *Director*.

Both Shambles buildings were demolished in the nineteenth century. Smith's design was for a modest pedimented building with stone angle quoins and a turret. The borough coat of arms set in a rococo cartouche was carved by Jeremiah Hargrave for £7 7s. 0d. The Fish

Shambles was a series of open arches enclosing an elongated octagon, a building for which Middleton was paid £105.

By chance the unknown builder of Tymperon's Hospital (c. 1731) selected an architectural motif that was to prove locally popular. The use of simple arcading was much favoured both by Andrea Palladio (1518-80) and his many English followers. An English edition of Palladio's designs including that of the Villa Emo had been published in 1715 by G. Leoni, followed in 1727 by Kent's publication of Lord Burlington's design for the school and almshouse at Sevenoaks. The latter is dominated by prolonged arcading. At Beverley the motif is repeated, over and over again during the eighteenth and nineteenth centuries, though always on a small scale (*figs.* 138-45).

The typical Queen Anne or Early Georgian facade was of two storeys crowned by a bold brick or timber cornice, and a steep flat — or pantiled roof pierced by dormers. To save expense, flat tiles were confined to those parts of the roof seen by the public. The rows of windows were closely spaced by later standards (*fig.* 102), and, when new, had leaded casements hung from stout oak mullions (or cross shaped mullions and transoms). Such casements were standard practice until c.1740-50, but thereafter they were rapidly replaced by the ubiquitous sliding sashes, so that few old casements now survive. Until 1972 there was one at the rear of 4 Wednesday Market and another can still be seen nearby at No. 15 (though its future is in doubt). On wider frontages symmetry was easily attained, with two or three windows on either side of the door, but a popular local alternative was the four bay front. Most doors were simple, resembling an extended window opening set within a projecting strip of brickwork (*fig.* 5).

Internally, the small, cubical rooms were usually wood panelled with, occasionally, the chimney-breast placed across an inner corner. The main staircase was fitted into a square well, with three short flights leading to the landing on the fourth side. The earlier type had closed strings, elaborately moulded (e.g. *figs.* 97, 107), but experiments were made with cantilevered flights. As a compromise, some staircases have flights with steps that project a few inches from a cellar or a cupboard wall, and at least one has 'steps' painted in *trompe l'oeil* on plain boarding (*fig.* 112). Most newel posts were square and were terminated by finials, but by 1709 columnar newels were becoming fashionable. The turned pine balusters were either based directly upon stone prototypes, e.g., at 30-32 Lairgate or were modifications of them (e.g. *figs.* 100, 111). The more expensive alternative was to have balusters with carved barley sugar twists. Good examples of the former pattern (not illustrated here) are at 15 Wednesday Market, 7-9 and 23 North Bar Within and of the latter at 3-5 Ladygate, 1 Norwood, 11 and 12-14 Butcher Row. Secondary staircases were more cramped and often ill lit, though quite often where they were seen or used by members of the family, they had handsome balustrades. As an economy the handrail was only moulded on the outer side (*c.f. sketch on right and fig.* 100).

Entrance and staircase hall floors were stone flagged, with either random slabs, or in squares laid diamondwise. At 3-5 Ladygate the slabs are alternately soft pink and green. In halls only the dados were wood panelled, elsewhere in the house the rooms were fitted up with oak or pine bolection — moulded panelling, nailed on top of the basic wooden framework (*figs.* 95, 117). Similar but bolder mouldings framed fireplace openings and overmantels (some of the latter retaining their contemporary paintings of fanciful landscapes) (*figs.* 96, 113). There are three such at 54 Keldgate and another at 11 St. John Street. Where only the simplest panelling could be afforded, it was composed of roughly planed vertical boarding, butt jointed, or with joints concealed by thin vertical strips of moulded wood. The typical door of the period had three panels, two approximately square, the central one a narrow rectangle. Sometimes, as an economy, mouldings were confined to one side, or, as at the now demolished Globe Inn in Ladygate, a door could be made from a single sheet of wood. Stout wrought iron H or HL shaped hinges were nailed to the door surface, a necessity where doors were thin.

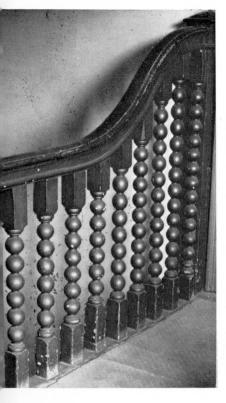

Staircases c. 1690-1720. FIGS. 106 (above left) & 108 (above right) *No. 71 Walkergate. The right hand balusters of* FIG. 108 *are replacements of 1833. When seen from below the 'bobbin turning' in* FIG. 106 *resembles the more expensive hand-carved spirals shown in* FIG. 112. FIG. 107 (above centre) *No. 51 Keldgate c. 1700.* FIG. 109 (below left) *Cross Keys Hotel, No. 8 Lairgate.* FIG. 110 (below centre) *No. 26 Eastgate. These two staircases together with those at No. 28 Eastgate and No. 46 Saturday Market were probably once in the Hotham House, Eastgate (c. 1716-21) which was demolished in 1766.* FIG. 111 (below right)   *Lairgate Hotel Nos. 30-32 Lairgate. A secondary staircase c. 1690.*

The front door usually led into a narrow vestibule which is separated from the staircase compartment by a panelled arch (*figs.* 104, 112). The principal rooms faced the street while the servants quarters projected into the yard or garden. The dining room and 'common parlours' were on the ground floor, above which would be the drawing room and the 'best chambers'. Sometimes, as at 7 Hengate, the drawing room consisted of adjoining 'parlours' linked by tall double doors. Where space permitted small closets off the principal rooms were a desirable amenity.

Behind the biggest houses there was sometimes enough space for a formal garden. In 1724 Wyndham Knatchball and his cousin visited Beverley and were shown 'the beautifull Gardens of Mr Miser, wch in 4 acres of Ground contain great variety of Avenues of Firrs, of Parterres of Statues; & also of Arbours, Seats & Vases in Trilliage Work; besides two Seats one of Ionic pillasters, the other of Doric Pillars painted by Parmentier'. (These gardens were thoroughly remodelled in the landscape manner leaving no trace of the garden temples, and a search for their foundations during current building operations produced only medieval pottery sherds and a skeleton.)

Until the building of the Hotham House in 1716-21 (and the publication of contemporary architectural treatises that laid stress upon architectural 'regularity') the early eighteenth century master builders were not over much concerned with strict symmetry, but Colen Campbell's design for Sir Charles Hotham's mansion included an east-west vista from the front porch through a columned screen across the saloon into the formal garden beyond, and an axial vista the full width of the garden front that culminated in a broad niche on the north wall. In conformity with correct Palladian usage, Campbell also took as great care with the overall proportions of the house as with those of the individual rooms. Thus the centre block was almost a cube in both plan and elevation, and its

FIG. 112   *Staircase No. 7 Hengate c.* 1708-09.

facade was a simplification of that of Lindsey House, Lincoln's Inn Fields, which, according to Campbell, was a work of Inigo Jones. The interior fittings included a mahogany and cedar grand staircase, gilded carving and marble chimneypieces, and the main rooms boasted a display of the Orders. The surviving evidence indicates that the interiors, for which the Thorntons were paid over £1,000, were closer to the Baroque style of their work at Wentworth Castle or Beningbrough Hall, than to the Palladian designs of Campbell. In 1766 Hotham House was bought and demolished by a group that included Thomas Wrightson and Dr. John Johnston, and the demolition materials can still be traced in houses associated with both men (*figs.* 110, 115, the carved fragment shown in *fig.* 114, retains traces of the original gilding).

The formality displayed at the Hotham House found minor echoes in houses built c. 1730 —c. 1750. Pedimented centrepieces and real or dummy Palladian doors can be seen at 62 North Bar Without and 51 Keldgate, and, by a discreet mixing of bolection moulded panels and those of simpler character, even a modest room could be made handsome (*figs.* 120, 122). There was also a greater attention to the 'correct' use of cornices: simple Doric for entrance halls, Ionic (with dentils or simple modillions) and Corinthian or

FIG. 113 (top left) *Wood and marble chimneypiece at Nos. 18-20 North Bar Within c. 1700.* FIGS. 114, 115 (left centre) *Re-used fragments of carving by W. Thornton from the Hotham House.* FIG. 116 (below) *Hotham House, Eastgate, designed by Colen Campbell for Sir Charles Hotham as shown on plate 87 of Vol. 2, Campbell's 'Vitruvius Britannicus'. For Plans see Back End Paper.*

Composite (with more elaborate modillions) for reception rooms, each type, of course, more expensive than the last. The Doric type is a commonplace, the second can be seen in (e.g. *figs*. 120, 122, 123) and the third can be glimpsed through the shop windows of 15 and 43-45 North Bar Within. The former was once the home of Sir Francis Boynton, the latter was the well-known Tiger Inn where, from time to time, the Corporation held civic banquets. At the same period, by combining entrance and staircase halls into one generous two-storeyed compartment, the visitor was greeted by a display of opulence not possible with the earlier layout (*fig*. 128).

The town's builders were reluctant to exchange the solid dignity of the Palladian style for the lighter hearted Rococo manner so strongly advocated by the authors of mid-eighteenth century pattern books such as those of Thomas Johnson or Thomas Chippendale, though the Rococo details found upon ceilings, cartouches, and carved panels, are evidence of an acquaintance with such works (*figs*. 155, 156).

In price, pattern books could be bought for anything from a few shillings to as many guineas. The more astute craftsmen realised that by subscribing to a volume they not only bought the work more cheaply but advertised themselves through the printed lists of subscribers. They also realised that the likely patronage to be found in Beverley was insufficient to provide a living for carvers, and 'the better sort of plasterers', for whom Hull or York were better centres. Thus, for example, the Hargraves migrated to Hull, and the best plasterers such as Cortese or Henderson lived in York (*figs*. 157,158).

The tendency to build or rebuild with three storeys rather than two, and to display carving in greater abundance were outward signs of mid-Georgian prosperity. The Corporation remodelled the Guildhall, and the gentry subscribed toward the New Assembly Rooms designed by John Carr of York (*fig*. 165), and in both William Middleton had a hand. The change of scale can be seen by comparing the Dings (rebuilt 1740-58) (*fig*. 9) and No. 39 Market Place (rebuilt by Matthew Harland in 1761-62) (*fig*. 76). Harland contracted to erect 'a handsome stock brick front, sash windows and an attick towards the Market Place'. The word 'handsome' was not used in connection with the Dings project, where it was thought enough to build uniformly. This change of scale and style is also apparent in the rebuilding of two Featherstone properties, 48 and 56 North Bar Without, the former rebuilt between 1726 and 1734, the latter completed in 1765. One opens directly on to the pavement, the other stands well back, one has panelled rooms and a carved pine staircase of Wrightson type, the other rooms that needed wallpapering, and a staircase of stone and wrought iron (*fig*. 223). This withdrawal from the street frontage is also found at Norwood House (c. 1765), Walkergate House (c. 1770), and most conspicuously, Lairgate Hall (c. 1760-65). It coincided with the fashion for informal landscape gardening, a style that demanded space which could only be obtained by the purchase (often over a prolonged period) of numerous adjoining properties.

Craftsmen with little or no working capital were understandably hesitant to embark upon speculative building, though, like Peter Duke in 1736 (when he proposed to rebuild 34-36 North Bar Within) (*fig*. 79) they could sometimes arrange a mortgage. It was preferable to build for those who were financially sound, and from the profits thus obtained, to venture cautiously, often by picking a suitable business partner where necessary, or by diversifying in such a way that both skills and materials were concentrated within a single firm. In the earlier eighteenth century both the Ellinors and the Wrightsons had just such combinations of skills, and the Wrightson interests in timber, brickmaking and lime-burning were further assets. Among business partnerships those of Middleton and Worlington, and Priestman and Clarkson may be noted here. All indulged in speculative building. Thus in 1754 Thomas Wrightson bought 'Daunts House', and on its site erected the present 17-19 Toll Gavel and 88, 90-92 Walkergate (*fig*. 147). The last named were built as a theatre, but Wrightson quickly converted the building into two houses. Five years later, in 1759, Middleton purchased 'Englebert Hall' in Highgate and on a portion of its frontage built No. 2 Highgate. In 1756 and in the same street William Priestman, carpenter and Joseph Clarkson, bricklayer put up a large house ('where a maltkin stood') which later became a public house known as the Black Swan (*fig.* 185). For much of the 1760's, Middleton was chiefly engaged in building for the public authorities (*figs.* 12 & 154), but in 1769 he bought up some cottages in Butcher Row and on their site built the present Nos. 16-18, another property of generous dimensions. A comparison of the known works of the Wrightsons and those of Middleton gives point to the remark of Dr. Nicholas Barbon (c. 1640-98) who could tell the trade of a master builder by looking at a facade 'Some being set out with fine brickwork rubbed and gaged, were the Issue of a master bricklayer. If stone coyned, jamb'd, and fascia'd, of a stone mason.' etc. The Wrightsons, as brickmakers, liked moulded brick cornices, but as joiners liked handsome staircases too (*figs.* 6, 133). Middleton's documented houses all have timber cornices as befitted a carpenter and joiner (*fig.* 10).

The typical mid and late Georgian facade has fewer, larger, more widely spaced sash windows, the sash bars being thick and of oak, or thin and of pine (*figs.* 76, 179-80). It had become standard practice to lay bricks in Flemish bond with fine white lime putty joints to show off the bond pattern to advantage. Window arches (some with stone keystones) (*figs.* 148) were similarly pointed (many having dummy 'joints' added solely for aesthetic effect). Where owners could afford it, the roofing material was Westmorland slate, which was longer lasting, and which needed a shallower pitch. During the 1760's wood or stucco panelling was retained as a foil for the double decker chimneypieces then at the height of fashion (*figs.* 120, 152, 190). In new houses with landscape gardens, the principal rooms were confined to the ground floor, otherwise the front room on the first floor retained its pre-eminence. About 1756, however, Isaac Ware noted a new phenomenon, the building of 'great rooms'.

> 'In houses which have been some time built, and which have not an out of proportion room, the common practice is to build one to them; this always hangs from one end, or sticks to one side of the

FIGS. 117 (opposite top), 119 (opposite below), 120 (above), 121 (below) *No. 51 Keldgate.* FIG. 118 (opposite centre) *Plates 52-53 from W. Kent's 'Designs of Inigo Jones', Vol. 2, 1727. About 1740 the Wilks' family united two separate dwellings creating a music room (FIGS 120-121) in the western portion to the right of FIG. 119. The front door is based upon a design by Batty Langley dated 1739.* FIG. 107 & FIG. 117 *show interiors c. 1700.* FIG. 121 *For economy the carving was strictly confined to the front of the chimney breast.*

FIGS. 122 (above) & 124 (below right) '*Ash Close*', *No. 62 North Bar Without. Built for N. Grantham c. 1732. In FIG. 122 note the mixture of bolection and raised and fielded panelling.* FIG. 123 (below left) *No. 19 North Bar Within. Panelled room on the first floor, c. 1740.* FIG. 125 (opposite left) *No. 30 Highgate c. 1720. Probably re-windowed to save Window Tax.* FIG. 126 (opposite centre) *No. 3 Newbegin. A Mid Georgian house with a Victorian Classical front door case.* FIG. 127 (opposite right) *No. 17 Highgate, c. 1760. The cornice duplicates that formerly on No. 39 Saturday Market.*

house, and shows to the most careless eye that, though fastened to the walls, it does not belong to the building. . . . The custom of routs has introduced this absurd practice. Our forefathers were pleased with seeing their friends as they chanced to come, and with entertaining them when they were there. The present custom is to see them all at once, and to entertain none of them; this brings in the necessity of a *great room* which is opened only on such occasions and which loads and generally discredits the rest of the edifice'.

An excellent example of a 'great room' is the Music Room of 51 Keldgate described as 'lately rebuilt' in 1753's, and to a less extent John Carr's extention to Lairgate Hall and the Regency library wing of Norwood House merit a similar description (*figs*. 119, 151).

The generously carved 'continued' chimneypiece in the Music Room at 51 Keldgate is one of the few survivors, but there are others at the Guildhall, Lairgate Hall and Nos. 11 and 39 Saturday Market. The latter two are by the same carver, who evidently delighted in the unorthodox, for at No. 39 he encrusted real minerals, pebbles and sea shells on to the rockwork beneath the bridge on the centre tablet and on the grotto that crowns the overmantel (*figs*. 136, 190-91). The carvers also busied themselves on numerous doorcases (e.g. *figs*. 169, 174). As wallpapers became more readily available, however, the use of panelling (and with it, of double decker chimneypieces) became less frequent. Rooms at 19 North Bar Within (*fig*. 123), 28 Saturday Market and Lairgate Hall all retain late examples of raised and fielded panelling. This transitional phase, from Palladian-Rococo to 'Adam' is best illustrated in the two mansions, Norwood House and Lairgate Hall. The former was built for Jonathan Midgley, an attorney, the latter for one of the Pennyman family. Norwood House had a centre block and two somewhat diminutive wings (*figs*. 165, 167. Its authorship is unknown, but on stylistic grounds an attribution to John Carr is the least likely. Both Thomas Atkinson of York (1729-98) and the Lightolers were well known to Midgley, but so too were Joseph Page of Hull and William Middleton. It is possible that either Atkinson and the Lightolers produced a plan and elevation, leaving the finishing in the hands of a competent man such as Page. T. Lightoler (which one is not stated), with William and John Halfpenny and Robert Morris, re-issued Colen Campbell's design for a ceiling at Compton Place, Eastbourne' as plate 79 of their *Modern Builder's Assistant* (1757 edition), a design that is a likely source for Midgley's Drawing Room ceiling (*fig*. 152). The door cases are

derived from a plate in Kent's *Inigo Jones*, but the charming if rather churchy overmantel panel is as characteristic of the 1760's as are the papier maché ornaments in the entrance hall and the octagonal glazing of the garden door in the staircase hall. Such a glazing bar pattern recurs on plate 69 of the *Modern Builder's Assistant*. The garden front is quite devoid of the Gibbs' Palladian adornments that were felt to be indispensable for the Norwood facade (*figs.* 151, 171).

If certain decorative details of Norwood House were rather old fashioned, the exterior of Lairgate Hall was exaggeratedly so. (Indeed the house looks little different from Newbegin House, a resemblance that must surely be intentional) (*figs.* 101, 160). When first built c. 1760 there were two more windows, that were, like the front door, replaced by the present Regency porch. The best of the earlier interiors is that now used as the Town Clerk's room on the first floor. The secondary staircase is contemporary. About 1770 Sir James Pennyman, the then owner (he was Mayor of the Borough in 1772), added the present reception rooms almost certainly to Carr's designs. The dining room ceiling repeats that designed in 1771 by Carr for the Great Dining Room at Thirsk Hall (*figs.* 158-59), and the stucco wall panelling repeats that at both Thirsk and that formerly in York Assize Courts, another undisputed work of Carr's. Moreover, a bedroom cornice at Lairgate Hall repeats one at Bootham Hospital (1773) also by Carr, among several other motifs typical of that architect. The Thirsk Hall ceiling was executed by James Henderson of York for £74 12s. 4d. Two finely carved wooden chimney-pieces remain (*fig.* 196), but the original marble one in the Chinese Drawing Room was removed prior to the sale of the house to Beverley Corporation, and another, remarkably similar to it, was given to the corporation to complete the restoration of the room. The hand-painted Chinese wallpaper (*fig.* 166), has panels that duplicate some at Nostell Priory (supplied in 1771 by Thomas Chippendale at a cost of 15/- per piece). The fine stucco ceiling, the rich mahogany doors and carved woodwork are an excellent interpretation of the Adam style that Carr had seen develop when he and his rival Robert Adam had been employed at Harewood. Much of the luxurious furniture of Lairgate Hall was sold by auction in 1781.

Sir James Pennyman also built 6-8 Newbegin whose doorcases are also good examples of the Adam manner. They are nearly identical to others at 3 Hengate (*fig.* 174), 1 Saturday Market (by William Middleton) and 55-63 North Bar Within. The latter terrace (*fig.* 78), was built for the Yarborough family who inherited the Beverley estates of the Wartons in 1775. About the same time 30-32 Lairgate was remodelled internally (*figs.* 161, 192) and externally (the top floor of the Lairgate front is of this date). The small scale, finely cut detail characteristic of the Adam period was inevitably expensive, though if cast lead, Coade stone, or 'composition' ornaments were employed the cost could be much reduced. For example 'composition' Adam urns by such firms as Wolstenholme of Gillygate, York, cost 8s.—9s. a dozen, and elegant swags or 'drops' 6d. and 3d. a piece. William Middleton used such motifs on chimneypieces at the Bar House and at 72-74 Lairgate (*fig.* 183). Similar work can be seen at 86-88 Lairgate, 12 Hengate and 8 Wednesday Market, the last named 'newly built' by Robert Brown, carpenter, in 1785. The staircase shown in *fig.* 163, has a whorl inlaid into the top of the handrail at the foot of the stairs. At this period balusters had become attenuated columns set beneath a slim mahogany or pine handrail (e.g. *figs.* 175, 178). Less ambitious interiors still had dado panelling, fine brass locks and attractive wooden chimneypieces, within which would be cast-iron 'Adam' grates by firms such as the Carron Company (*fig.* 168). The finely moulded joinery, and prettily patterned wallpapers and textiles set off the fine mahogany furniture then being made in considerable quantities in Hull and Beverley, by firms such as the Walkers or the Hunsleys.

FIG. 128 (opposite) *'The Elms', No. 29 North Bar Without. Probably by W. Wrightson, c. 1730-40. Note the pattern created by the projecting ends of the treads and risers, c.f. figs. 129-34.*

FIG. 129 (above left)   *Staircase designed by Abraham Swan in 'The British Architect' (1745). c.f. the Ionic column newel*
FIG. 130. FIG. 130 (above centre)   *Carved staircase perhaps by W. Wrightson c. 1750, Highgate House, Wednesday Market.*
FIG. 131 (above right)   *No. 11 Saturday Market, built for J. Hall, clockmaker, c. 1755 perhaps by T. Wrightson.* FIG. 132
(below left)   *No. 19 North Bar Within. Also in the style of the Wrightsons who had a financial interest in the property.*
FIG. 133 (below centre)   *No. 35 North Bar Within. Built by W. Wrightson in 1740.* FIG. 134 (below right)   *Newbegin Bar
House. Built by W. Wrightson 1744-46. Both No. 35 North Bar Within and Newbegin Bar House have white 'dots' inset into
the hall floor.*

PLAN OF LAIRGATE HALL (as existing)

A—Chinese Drawing Room (*figs.* 166, 170).

B—Dining Room (*fig.* 158).

C—Staircase Hall (*fig.* 161).

D—Former Servants' Wing now partially converted into office accommodation.

E—Principal Reception Room before the addition of rooms A and B.

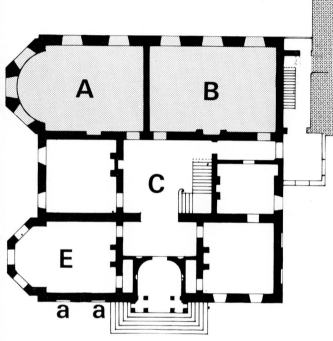

FIG. 135 *Doors to Sedan Chair House, Newbegin Bar House,* 1744-46.

The plan above reflects the change in attitude toward garden design—the older Appleyard family house, St. Giles, fronted on to Lairgate. Its Pennyman successor was inset into a small landscape park acquired by lease and purchase. The views extended east over St. Margaret's Close, south and west to Keldgate and Westwood. Sir James Pennyman preferred the latter. The east facing windows (a–a) were blocked up and a new bay added to room E. The bay motif was repeated in A in the extension of c. 1771. In order to achieve the widest panorama, the servant's block was attached to the north-west corner, a situation often favoured by 'Capability' Brown.

FIG. 136 (right) *Panelled interior, No. 11 Saturday Market c. 1755.*

FIG. 137 (below) *East side of North Bar Without. No. 48 built for R. Featherstone between 1726 and 1734.*

The patches of darker coloured brickwork on No. 48 (partly hidden by the shutters) indicate the positions of the former window openings. Originally there were two windows to the left of the door and probably three to the right. The painted plaster cornice is of a type once common in Beverley. (For an Edwardian version of the motif see York County Savings Bank, 65-66 Saturday Market.)

FIG. 138 (opposite) *W. Tymperon's Hospital 'about to be built' in 1731.*

FIG. 139 (above left)   *Ann Routh's Hospital, Keldgate, 1748-50. Designed by J. Moyser, built by T. Wrightson.*   FIG. 140 (below left)   *Detail of engraving of Sevenoaks Almshouse, designed by Lord Burlington.*   FIG. 141 (bottom left)   *Railway Goods Warehouse probably designed by G. T. Andrews.*   FIG. 142 (top right)   *No. 78 Lairgate. Mid Georgian frontage to a builder's yard.*   FIG 143 (above right)   *Victorian extension to Ann Routh's Hospital.*   FIG. 144 (below right)   *Nos. 45-47 Keldgate. Early 19th C.*   FIG. 145 (bottom right)   *Design for the Southern Block, Beverley Workhouse, Minster Moorgate, by J. Walker, 1838.*

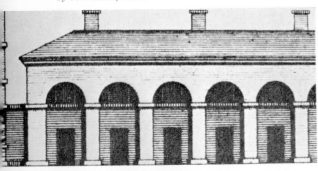

Fig. 146 (above left) *Walkergate House c. 1770.* Fig. 147 (below left) *Nos. 88, 90-92 Walkergate built by T. Wrightson c. 1754. The latter built as a theatre.* Fig. 148 (above right) *Cross Keys Hotel, Nos. 4-8 Lairgate. No. 6 c. 1855, No 8. Mid 1760's.* Fig. 149 (below right) *No. 38 Highgate. Perhaps altered by J. Robinson c. 1740. (The former Blue Coat School).* Fig. 150 (bottom right) *Nos. 59-65 Flemingate. Mid and Late Georgian ribbon development similar to that in outlying villages.*

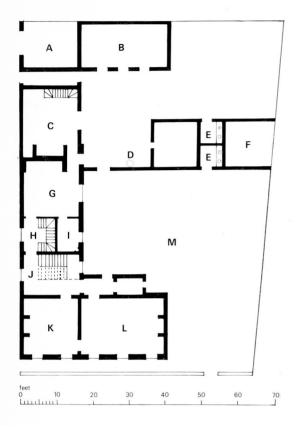

feet
0   10   20   30   40   50   60   70

WILLIAM WRIGHTSON'S CONTRACT & PLAN for NEWBEGIN BAR HOUSE

The original contract and the counterpart lease are now deposited with the East Riding County Records Office. Calendar Nos.: D.D.B.C./19/7 P.R./651/A/46.

The contract and the plan (redrawn) are reproduced here as examples of contemporary documentation (the staircase as executed differs slightly from that shown on Wrightson's plan and the intended brick wall on the West front, shown in outline on the adjacent plan, was replaced by iron railings). It is worth noting that in c. 1779 the interior of the house was substantially remodelled during the tenancy of Mr. Dobson (*see* p. 47).

A   Sedan Chair House
B   Stables
C   Back Kitchen
D   Pump
E   Necessary Houses
F   Manure Hole
G   Kitchen
H   Back Stairs
I   Pantry
J   Staircase Hall
K   Common Dining Room
L   Dining Room
M   Garden

Articles of Agreement made concluded and fully Agreed upon Between the Mayor Aldermen and Burgesses of the Town of Beverley in the County of York of the One part and William Wrightson of the Said Town of Beverley Carpenter of the other part as followeth that is to say.

The Said William Wrightson doth hereby for himself his Executors Administrators and Assigns covenant promise and grant to and with the Sd. Mayor Aldermen Burgesses their Successors Assigns in manner following. That is to say That the Said William Wrightson his Executors Admnrs or Assigns or some of them for the Considerations here in after mentioned shall and will on or before the Twenty ninth Day of September next in and upon a certain piece or parsell of Ground adjoining the South Side of Newbegin Barr in Beverley aforesd. And now in the occupation of John Author his Undertenants made erect build Set up and cover in One messuage Tenement or dwellinghouse Stable Chairhouse & Other Buildings pursuant to a plan delivered to the Sd. Mayor Aldermen and Burgesses and Annext to a counter part of a Lease of the Sd. premises bearing even Date herewith and granted ffrancis Best Esquire And Also shall and will finish & compleat the Same on or before the Twenty Fifth Day of March which will be in the Year of our Lord One Thousand Seven Hundred and fforty Six in a Workmanlike manner And according to the Description Dimentions and Scantlings of the Said Buildings and materials hereinafter mentioned To witt. To Sink Archover with Brick and divide Two Cellars under both the Staircases to be paved with comon Brick and Oak-Steps dessending there into The ffront and rear Walls of the new dwelling house to be Brick and half Thick from foundation to the Pann The West ffront Wall to be wrought with the Stock Brick with a Brick Cornice All the Other Walls belonging the Buildings And the Partitions in the low Rooms to be Brick in length The partitions in the Upper Stories a Brick in Breadth wrought with Comon Brick. The Low Story Nine foot and an half high And the Chambers Nine feet high clear the panwood Lintells and Sleeper Wood of good Oak a Sufficient Usual Scantling The Sparrs of Sawn red ffirwood four Inches by five Inches All the Roof to be covered with Hollow Tyles after a common manner To place Ten Oak Sash Windows in the West ffront aboiut Six feet high Sash And one in the Staircase & All Glazed with new Castle Crown Glass with ffree stone Soaks in the West ffront the Bottom part of the Sd. Sash Windows to slide All the Out Door and Window frames to be of Seasoned Oak of a Sufficient and proportionable Dimention to be glazed wtih new Castle Crown Glass wrought in Lead And Iron Casements where needfull The iron works for the floors & Roof - to be good and Sufficient All the Doors to the Rooms to be framed and hung with Sufficient Locks Bolt Joints Hinges and Snecks where needfull, among which Locks are to be ffive Brass Locks about Seven Shillings and Sixpence a piece . . . The Joists of Sawn red ffir Seven Inches by three Inches an an half about ffourteen Inches distant The Garret ffloors to be laid with common Deals the Chambers and dining Room to be Wainscotted with good common Gauged Deals clear of Sap - the best dining Room to be Wainscotted with pedestall and Dentill Cornice And the Other Dining Room to be Wainscotted with a fashionable plain Cornice and Closets taken off both Sides of the Chimney The Vestible to be Stucoed the best Stairs to be carried up after a neat good manner The Back Stairs to the Garrets after a Common Manner - Two ffront Chambers to be finished and Surrounded with Cornice and Plinth One Chamber to be hung with Paper at Sixpence a yard And the other Two Chambers and Two Closets with paper at fourpence a yard The Windows in the ffront Chambers to be finished with Seats and Shutts all the rest of the Windows with plain Deal Seats And Architraves Two of the Garrets to be underdrawn All the Room Tops to be thick lathed and finished with Lime & Hair And all the Walls in the kitchen Chambers over them, and Back = Stair Case with Lime and Hair the best Stair Case with plain Stucoe the ffloor of the Vestible to be covered with Diamond fflagg paving the kitchens pantryes and passage with Stock Brick ffloors All the whole building to be painted three times over with Common Colours, to fix in the four West ffront Rooms Stone Architraves & fflag Hearths to fix Shelves in the Pantry Closets and Cellar and pinns where necessary The Stable to be Chambered Over and made into four Standings with Racks and Mangers and paved with ffield Cobbles A Well to be Sunk and a lead pump to be fixed and Cased All pump yard and passage as ffar as the Coalhole to be paved with ffield Cobbles Two mannure plases or Dungholes to be made and Two Privies or Houses of Convenience The Coal hole to be finished according to the plann And a Wall to be continued from the Same to the house Seven feet high Also a wall to be built before the West ffront Six foot high caped with Brick on Edge To be made four Low Room Three Chamber Two Garret and One Closet Chimney of a proportionate dimention to their respective Rooms the first ffloor to be about three Steps above the Street The old Buildings to Stand as the plan directs but to be Altered as therein set fforth Poll Spouts to be fixed on the South Side as far as the kitchin South Side of the Butlers pantry The Two Closets over the Two pantries to be hung with Common paper.

And the Said Mayor Alderman and Burgesses in Consideration of the Said Buildings to be erected and finished in manner aforesd. do hereby for themselves their Successors & Assigns covenant and agree to pay or cause to be paid unto the said William Wrightson his Executors Minors and Assigns the full Sum of Three hundred & fifteen pounds of good & lawfull money of Great Britain in manner following To witt One Hundred pounds part thereof on about the first day of May next ensuing One Hundred Pounds more on or about the Eleventh day of November . . . next ensuieing And One Hundred and fifteen pounds Residue and in full payment of the Sd. Sum of three hundred and fifteen pounds on or about the first day of May which will be in the Year our Lord One Thousand Seven Hundred & forty Six. In Witness - whereof the said Mayor Aldermen & Burgesses have here unto caused the comon Seal of the sd. Town of Beverley to be affixed And also the said William Wrightson hath hereunto for his Hand and Seal the Twenty ffirst . . . Day of March One Thousand Seven Hundred and fforty ffour.

Sealed and delivered being first duely Stampt in presence of

WILLIAM WRIGHTSON.

FIG. 151 (opposite) *Garden front of Norwood House c. 1765-70 except for Library block to the left built c. 1825 for W. Beverley.* FIG. 152 (below) *Norwood House, drawing room. Stucco work in the style of J. Page of Hull. The ceiling design is based upon one for Compton Place, Eastbourne, Sussex, designed by Colen Campbell. For detail of overmantel, see back of book jacket.*

FIG. 153 (right)   *East wall of the Magistrate's room in the Guildhall. Designed and executed by W. Middleton 1762-64. The contemporary chairs are by W. Thompson of Beverley.*

FIG. 154 (below)   *The Courtroom in the Guildhall by W. Middleton and G. Cortese 1762-64. The columns in the foreground were removed from Beverley Minster in 1826.*

FIG. 155 (opposite above left)   *Detail from Plate 173 of T. Chippendale's 'Director' 1762.*

FIG. 156 (opposite above right)   *Detail of carving by Edmund Foster of Hull, c.f. figs. 154-55.*

FIG. 157 (opposite below left)   *Detail of Courtroom ceiling designed and executed by G. Cortese.*

Ground floor and first floor plan of Guildhall (opposite bottom right).

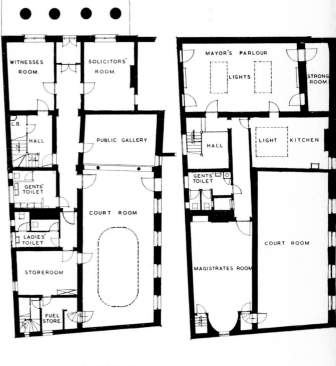

GROUND FLOOR PLAN   FIRST FLOOR PLAN.

FIG. 158 (above left)   *Detail of dining room ceiling, Lairgate Hall, c. 1771, probably designed by J. Carr of York and carried out by J. Henderson of York.*   FIG. 159 (above right)   *Detail of the Great Dining Room ceiling, Thirsk Hall. Designed by J. Carr of York and carried out by J. Henderson of York at a cost of £74 12s. 4d.*   FIG. 160 (below)   *Lairgate Hall from S.E. The main block c. 1760. The bay windows are later additions. The front porch is Early 19th C.*

FIG. 161 (above left) *Lairgate Hall. The staircase hall probably designed by J. Carr of York c. 1771.* FIG. 162 (below left) *Lairgate Hotel, the main staircase c. 1775.* FIG. 163 (above right) *No. 8 Wednesday Market by R. Brown, carpenter, c. 1785.* FIG. 164 (below right) *No. 3 North Bar Within. Staircase c. 1815.*

FIG. 165 (above)   *Norwood looking towards Hengate c. 1907. The projecting porch on the left was of c. 1670. To its right a house by A. Bennison, architect, of Hull c. 1815. In the centre, the Assembly Rooms, designed by J. Carr and built by W. Middleton 1761-63, all now demolished. To the right Norwood House before the alterations to the wings.*   FIG. 166 (below left)   *Lairgate Hall, east wall of the Chinese drawing room c. 1771. The chairs are by W. Thompson c.f. fig. 153.*
FIG. 167 (below right)   *Centre block of Norwood House.*

FIG. 168 (opposite)   *No. 3 Hengate.   An interior of 1778.*

FIG. 169 (above left)   *Entrance doorway. No. 56 North Bar Without, 1765.*   FIG. 170 (above centre)   *Drawing room door, Lairgate Hall, probably by Carr of York c. 1771.*   FIG. 171 (above right)   *Garden doorway, Norwood House. Note octagonal glazing and the stout iron grilles.*   FIG. 172 (below left)   *Doorway, Bar Chambers, North Bar Within by W. Middleton 1793-94.*   FIG. 173 (below centre)   *No. 22 Hengate. Late Georgian door and windows (with original shutters).* FIG. 174 (below right)   *No. 3 Hengate. Doorway, 1778.*

In the earlier eighteenth century, Highgate was full of 'shops' — there was one row of at least eleven — but they may not have had shop fronts as such. The latter, with bay or bow windows were a mid-Georgian development. The Town Council reluctantly permitted these protruding windows to encroach upon the pavements for a yearly rent of at least 6d. The earliest surviving windows differ little from their domestic counterparts, and like them had hinged wooden shutters (*fig.* 199). Later Georgian shop fronts were bows rather than bays, with integral doorways and shutter boxes (*figs.* 200-3, 207).   Gradually as glass became cheaper, pane sizes increased, and the sash bars were reduced in number (*figs.* 205-6, 272).   The horizontal ones were the first to be eliminated, then from about 1880, the more prosperous shopkeepers indulged in plate glass windows to the full width of the front.

The earlier shop fronts had little space for lettering.   Most signs were therefore either painted upon projecting boards that swung from iron brackets, or were carved symbols appropriate to the trade concerned.   Though both types are still used to advertise public houses (e.g. *fig.* 173), only a few shops retain their early shop signs. A carved 'Red Indian' (a tobacconist's sign) is preserved at 34 Toll Gavel, and the former pharmacy at 44 Toll Gavel (*fig.* 208), is still adorned with its original snake-wreathed columns.

The original version of this drawing for alterations to 41a Saturday Market (above) was submitted to the Council in 1870. It amply illustrates the switching of bow windows from ground to first floor. The original drawing shows the new bays more prominently and the still existing Georgian windows faintly.

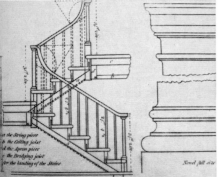

FIG. 175 (above left)   *No. 61 North Bar Within. A staircase of the 1770's perhaps by W. Middleton.*   FIG. 176 (above centre)   *No. 93 Minster Moorgate. A staircase by M. Constable, carpenter, 1758.*   FIG. 177 (above right)   *No. 25 Highgate. A staircase by W. Priestman, carpenter, 1756.*   FIG. 178 (middle left)   *Detail of staircase designed by W. Pain. 'Practical House Carpenter' Plate 64 c.f. fig. 175.* FIGS. 179-180 (below)   *Nos. 72-74 Lairgate. Built by W. & J. Middleton, 1797. If the vertical divisions of the ground and first floor windows (in fig. 179) had been wider than 12" each, double the amount of Window Tax would have been payable.*

FIG. 181 (top left) *Detail of lead statue of King Athelstan by W. Collins, 1781. The Jacobean or 'fancy' costume includes a rich lace collar and a 'Saxon' crown which made the figure resemble those in Garrick's stage productions of Shakespearean plays such as 'Richard III'. When new, fine sand was thrown onto the freshly painted surface to simulate stone.*

FIG. 182 (centre left) *Coadestone keystone, 1790. From No. 31 Butcher Row. There are copies of the Coade catalogue in the Library of the British Museum and in the Soane Museum.*

FIG. 183 (below centre left) *Detail of chimneypiece from No. 72 Lairgate with Wolstenholme 'composition' ornaments, 1797. A copy of one of the now rare catalogues of composition ornaments is in Du Pont Museum, Winterthur, Delaware, U.S.A.*

FIG. 184 (bottom left) *No. 93 Minster Moorgate built by M. Constable, 1758. Despite the prominence of the site Constable evidently preferred a free composition to one of greater formality c.f. William Wrightson's Newbegin Bar House, 1744-46.*

FIG. 185 (bottom right) *No. 25 Highgate built by Priestman & Clarkson c. 1756. Among its 18th C. owners were the de Lanceys, a French family who emigrated to America and became prominent members of New York society. As Loyalists they left New York when the British were defeated in the War of Independence (1776-83) but the name Delancey Street remains in what was to become the Whitechapel of New York.*

FIG. 186 (top left) *The Minster. 14th & 18th C. Window tracery, south Nave aisle.* FIG. 187 (top right) *St. Pierre, Caen, 14th C. Nave clerestory window.* FIG. 188 (centre left) *The Minster. A misericord, early 16th C.* FIG. 189 (bottom left) *Detail of a Netherlandish block book 'The Biblia Pauperum'. Mid 15th C. In the possession of the Victoria & Albert Museum.* FIG. 190 (bottom right) *Carved chimneypiece formerly at No. 39 Saturday Market, 1761.*

FIGS. 191-197 (opposite) *Details of carved chimneypieces.* FIG. 191 (top left) *Detail of fig. 190.* FIG. 192 (centre left) *30-32 Lairgate c. 1775.* FIG. 193 (below centre left) *20 New Walk (in marble) c. 1871.* FIG. 194 (bottom left) *43 North Bar Without by J. E. Elwell, 1880.* FIG. 195 (top right) *Norwood House, c. 1765-70.* FIG. 196 (centre right) *Lairgate Hall, probably designed by Carr of York.* FIG. 197 (below centre right) *'Uplands', Brimley. Carved by R. Reid in 1971 after a design by F. Johnson. The frieze was modelled upon one in Gt. Union Street, Hull, of c. 1803.* FIG. 198 (bottom right) *Carved oak overdoor panel, 6 North Bar Without, signed W. Thorley, for J. E. Elwell, 1892.*

Fig. 199 (top left) *Mid Georgian shop front. No. 28 Saturday Market, c.* 1765. Fig. 200 (centre left) *Later Georgian shop front. No.* 14 *Norwood.* Fig. 201 (bottom left) *Later Georgian shop fronts. Nos. 32-34 Saturday Market.* Fig. 202 (above right) *Later Georgian shop fronts (The Push). No.* 27 *Saturday Market.* Fig. 203 (below right) *Later Georgian shop front. No. 6 Eastgate.* Fig. 204 (opposite top left) *Detail of fig. 202. The carved brackets are a re-use of Early Georgian material.* Fig. 205 (opposite top right) *Early Victorian shop front. No.* 11 *Saturday Market. Inserted into a house built for J. Hall, clockmaker (see also figs.* 131 *and* 136). Fig. 206 (opposite centre right) *Mid Victorian shop fronts. Nos.* 99-101 *Walkergate, c.* 1860.

Fig. 207 (below left) *Late Georgian shop front. No. 25 Wood Lane.* Fig. 208 (below centre) *Detail of former Chemist's shop front. No. 44 Toll Gavel. The snakes are a symbol of Aesculapius, the God of Medicine, c. 1830.* Fig. 209 (below right) *Title page of a London Pharmacopoeia, published 1650.*

From the last years of the eighteenth century onward, perhaps the majority of houses have undergone substantial alteration, where rebuilding has not taken place. The most obvious change has been the transformation of the ground floor rooms of houses in the principal streets, into one or more shops. Sometimes this has meant only the renewal of the ground floor front wall, and the piercing of cross walls, to create a single space, timber or elegant cast iron columns being inserted to support the walls above. Georgian wooden columns can be seen at 7-9 North Bar Within, and Regency iron ones at 41a Saturday Market. A more drastic solution was to rebuild the whole frontage as at 15 North Bar Within or 52-53 Saturday Market (*fig.* 234). When this happened the corporation insisted that the bow window was removed, but, after some argument, permitted property owners to insert projecting bay windows into the floor above. Changes in private houses were less marked, but included remodelling the entrance doorway, the removal or concealment of old panelling and, most frequently, the renewal of chimneypieces. Only in less prosperous homes, or those where the landlord remained indifferent to changes in fashion, were the original fitments suffered to remain. Paradoxically the late Victorian revival of interest in the Georgian style resulted in the destruction of genuine Georgian work when the latter did not conform with the ideas of the revivalists. The most obvious example is the removal of the sash bars from the lower halves of windows. On the other hand the regular use of Georgian-type sash windows for much of the nineteenth century has helped to give the town a sense of visual unity (*figs.* 265-66). Why most architects and builders and their patrons rejected the Gothic Revival is not known, and even those that did venture into that style soon changed their tune, at least when working for local clients (compare *figs.* 247-55).

The Regency style did not quickly find adherents. The new white brick and stone Sessions House (designed in 1804 by Watson and Pritchett of York) has little of the 'gravitas' of similar buildings by Harrison of Chester or Sir Robert Smirke—it is 'Grecian' rather than Greek (*fig.* 230, *see also fig.* 268). The Gasworks gateway was closer to archaeological precedent and the Gas Company's earliest lamp standards (dated c.1824 and 1826) are an ingenious attempt to find a 'correct' answer to a new problem (*figs.* 225, 227). No other town can boast such an array of Georgian light fittings.

Within a decade the Greek mode became well established. In 1827 there were several proposals for a 'new street' to link Register Square and Well Lane. Edward Page's plan for the layout was accepted and architects and builders, including Charles Mountain, submitted a variety of elevations, none of which were built. Instead Cross Street (as it became) was lined by a group comprising the villa of Edward Page (now No. 11 (*fig.* 231)), a Baptist Chapel (now demolished), a Gentlemen's Club (now the County Record Office (*fig.* 233)), and a Mechanics Institute (now demolished), all put up between 1831 and 1842. Page adroitly disguised the truncated end of a cottage in Well Lane by the southern wing of his new house. These new stucco facades formed a homogeneous group with those in Register Square: the former Dispensary (now the Local Taxation Office), the house built for Charles Ross (now the County Library) and Charles Mountain's new front to the Guildhall (*fig.* 226). (The curving staircase of the 'Dispensary' incorporates demolition material from the Minster.) Greek Doric (*see fig.* 228), was used for all but the Mechanics Institute, which was Ionic, an order repeated by the unknown architect of the contemporary Savings Bank in Lairgate, No. 26-28 (*fig.* 232).

The 1840's may be considered a convenient watershed for our purposes. The railway, at first only to Hull and Bridlington, raised hopes of a prosperous future, especially for those with property leading to, or in the vicinity of the station. New industries such as the Crosskill iron and machinery works, the Tigar oil and colour works, now supplemented the staple industries of tanning, malting and brewing. Moreover the transport improvements of the previous decades made the movement of heavy goods much cheaper, making the excellent building stone of the West Riding available at an economic price.

Among the first of the new schemes was Edward and Gregory Page's new layout for the fields near the station. Railway Street (Albert Street in its earlier years) was to provide a handsome approach to Station Square (*fig.* 236). Gregory Page's own house (No. 13) was to be the model, but the later houses were all smaller and in the event, only the northern side was completed with any uniformity, while except for G. T. Andrews' station (*fig* 260), the architectual qualities of the Square itself are of a very modest order. At the other end of the town Marmaduke Lowson Whitton was slowly transforming the 'closes' between York Road and North Bar Without and, around 1853, had begun the terrace now known as Willow Grove (*fig*. 7). Whitton's brothers, James, an architect, and Robert, a stone and marble mason, assisted in the various schemes, the most unexpected of them the conversion of the former prison treadmill, turnkey's house and a block of men's cells into very respectable villas (now called Westfield, Norfolk St. *fig*. 268). The Whittons developed a belated version of the Regency style of their youth (*fig*. 237). The same was true of William Hawe (1822-97) who is said to have settled in Beverley as an architect about 1842. His earlier works have not been identified, though 52, 53 Saturday Market (built for Charles Hobson in 1853) and 1-3 Norwood Far Grove may, on stylistic grounds, be attributed to Hawe (*figs*. 234, 243).

Once, however, the Borough Council insisted upon the submission of plans in accordance with the terms of the Public Health Act of 1848, the pattern of Victorian building becomes much clearer. The worst crowding, and the shoddiest construction were no longer permitted. New streets had to be more uniform in width, with houses set back where possible to permit small gardens (*figs*. 263-67). Fortunately most of the plans submitted in compliance with the Act survive, and from them the houses built after the mid 1860's can be studied in considerable detail (e.g. *figs*. 272-73). Regrettably for the historian the Act did not specify that elevations must be submitted in all cases, though builders anxious to impress the councillors included elevations where they thought it worth their while. William Hawe's plans were always meticulously presented (*see* p. 106). He tinted the plans so that the areas allotted to the clients and to their servants were quickly distinguishable. He was also at pains to show innovations such as concrete floors, cavity walls, even door mat recesses. His practice included commercial and industrial buildings, terraces, villas and cottages, almost always in a 'fruity' Franco-German classical style. He liked Mansard roofs and rich stone or woodcarving, and his work has a general air of opulence. Even his cottages avoid the run of the mill, e.g. wider windows to let in more light on the ground floor and a deeply recessed front door to give a little extra privacy, as in Foster's Yard, Beckside (*fig*. 244). He was so convinced that his chosen style was the correct one that the Gothic trimming of the Bar House was swept away in favour of the present Italianate stuccowork. In later life Hawe took his stepson J. R. Foley into partnership (e.g. *figs*. 238, 246).

Hawe's biggest rivals were R. G. Smith and F. S. Brodrick. (The latter is not to be confused with Cuthbert Brodrick 'of Leeds' who, in 1861, was given an isolated commission here, the pair of houses shown in *fig*. 13 now 37 North Bar Within. Their bold scale is that of the city rather than that of a country town.) Smith and Brodrick stood with the Goths in the 'Battle of the Styles', though they readily embraced the 'Queen Anne' style associated with Norman Shaw (*figs*. 251, 255) when it was locally politic to do so, and at its best, their architecture shows a better grasp than that of Hawe (especially when Foley played a greater part in the practice). On the other hand Hawe's work was more consistent where his rivals were merely fashionable, for example in their juxtaposition of a heavy Gothic dining room next to an Adam drawing room in 'Oak House', North Bar Without. Both firms of architects preserved fragments of former buildings. Hawe re-sited the Georgian front doorcase of 11 Wednesday Market in Railway Street, and Smith and Brodrick re-used much of the earlier Georgian staircase at 43 North Bar Without, in the latter case perhaps at the insistence of their client James Edward Elwell, who probably designed and carved many of the internal fittings (*figs*. 254, 257-58). On his own account Elwell also re-modelled Nos. 4, 6, 8 North Bar Without (*fig*. 75).

None of the architects and builders so far mentioned could be deemed very adventurous in the context of Victorian architecture as a whole, but, though E. J. Sherwood's Salvation Army Barracks (of 1885) would scarcely rate a footnote with its external battlemented frontispiece, internally its

(*Continued on page* 103)

FIG. 210 (top left)   *Detail of Plate 4, I. & J. Taylor's 'Ornamental Ironwork' c. 1795, see fig. 213. Identical contemporary balustrades can be seen in Bagdale, Whitby. The pattern book version was probably inspired by William Kent's balustrading in the Great Hall at Holkham.*   FIG. 211 (top right)   *St. Mary's Church. Wrought iron altar probably by Hutton & Mainman, 1741-42.*   FIG. 212 (centre left)   *Detail of the black stained plywood model of the proposed gates, see fig. 214, which was put up for public inspection prior to manufacture.*   FIG. 213 (centre right)   *Detail of Late Georgian cast iron staircase, No. 62 North Bar Without, see fig. 210.*   FIG. 214 (below left)   *St. Mary's Church. Early 20th C. wrought iron churchyard gates, see also fig. 77.*   FIG. 215 (below centre)   *Norwood House. Mid Georgian wrought iron garden gate to the east of the house.*   FIG. 216 (below right)   *Detail of cast iron staircase at York Lodge, Seven Corners Lane. A house designed by Rawlins Gould of York, 1869. Identical balusters can or could be seen in The Registry Office, York, Oxford Gardens, North Kensington, and Oak Drive, Fallowfield, Manchester.*   FIG. 217 (top row left, opposite)   *Cast lead fanlight. No. 24 Lairgate c. 1798.*   FIG. 218 (top row right, opposite)   *Detail from J. Bottomley's 'Book of Designs', No. 3, 1793.*   FIG. 219 (second row left, opposite)   *Cast iron window frame, Railway warehouse, see fig. 141. An ingenious design that allowed the use of a standardised size of pane.*   FIG. 220 (second row right, opposite)   *Detail of Late Victorian cast iron down spout, Highgate House.*   FIG. 221 (centre left, opposite)   *Detail of brass cased lock by J. Tygar c. 1766. No. 46 Saturday Market.*

FIG. 222 (bottom far left)   *Cast iron staircase designed by C. Brodrick for No. 37 North Bar Within, see also fig. 13.*   FIG. 223 (bottom left)   *Wrought iron staircase. No. 56 North Bar Within c. 1765.*   FIG. 224 (bottom right)   *Detail of Plate 7, W. & J. Welldon's 'The Smiths' Right Hand' Part 2, 1765.*   FIG. 225 (bottom far right)   *Detail of Georgian gas lamp standard, made at the Thorncliffe Ironworks, Chapeltown, Sheffield, 1824. (The Crosskill foundry was not founded until 1825, after which date they made the new standards.)*

Fig. 226 (left) *The Guildhall. 'Greek' Doric portico by Chas. Mountain, Jnr., 1832. The lower part of the columns were left smooth to prevent unsightly damage — a frequent practice in Pompeii.* Fig. 227 (above right) *Main gateway of Beverley Gasworks built for J. Malam c. 1826. Similar to the gasworks' gateway at Oldham, Lancs.* Fig. 228 (below right) *Greek Doric Temple at Paestum, Nr. Naples c. 450 B.C.*

FIG. 229 (above left)   *Norwood House. Detail of 'Greek' pilaster capital of a marble chimneypiece c.* 1825.   FIG. 230 (above right)   *The Sessions House, North Bar Without by Watson & Pritchett of York c.* 1804-14. *Note the frieze of 'irons' on the portico ceiling*   FIG. 231 (below left)   *Detail of centre block, No.* 11 *Cross Street by E. Page,* 1834.   FIG. 232 (below right)   *The former Beverley Savings Bank,* 1843, *and Nos.* 30-32 *Lairgate.*   FIG. 233 (bottom)   *The County Record Office, formerly a Gentlemen's Club, Cross Street, c.* 1831.

FIG. 234 (above)   *Nos. 51-56 Saturday Market. Nos. 52-53 built for Charles Hobson, 1853, perhaps by W. Hawe. No. 54 is timber framed. Nos. 55 and 56 by W. Middleton, 1777 c.f. figs 8 and 9.*

FIG. 235 (below)   *Nos. 80-90 Lairgate. Early to Late Georgian houses. Nos. 86-88 built for A. Peacock, c. 1800-02.*

FIG. 237 (above)   *Nos. 5-45 North Bar Without, mostly by M. L. Whitton, 1853-63. Whitton intended to extend Park Terrace, Nos. 21-27, southwards. This would have meant the demolition of Nos. 13-19, the two-storied cottages in the centre of the picture. The scheme fell through and Whitton simply sub-divided the cottages to form the existing four. Though M. L. Whitton is usually named as the builder, he regularly called upon his architect brother James (of Lincoln), to design the plans and elevations.*

FIG. 236 (below)   *Nos. 13-33 Railway Street, laid out with Wilbert Grove and George Street in the late 1840's by Edward and Gregory Page. The latter's own much larger house is No. 13. Similar doorways can be seen at Nos. 64-66 North Bar Without. At first the new street was named after Prince Albert but the name was quickly changed to Railway Street.*

FIG. 238 (top left)   *The former Golden Ball Brewery by W. Hawe, c.* 1866.   FIG. 239 (above)   *No.* 20 *New Walk. Detail of staircase by W. Hawe,* 1876. (*The balusters show no change from their counterparts of a century earlier.*)   FIG. 240 (centre left)   *Nos.* 5-7 *Eastgate by W. Hawe,* 1871 (*see plan p.* 106). FIG. 241 (bottom left) *Nos.* 2-10 *New Walk by W. Hawe,* 1868-71.   FIG. 242 (bottom right)   *No.* 20 *New Walk. Detail of ceiling by W. Hawe,* 1876.

FIG. 243 (top left) *Nos. 1-3 Norwood Far Grove, probably by W. Hawe.*

FIG. 244 (top right) *Nos. 2-3 Fosters Yard, off Beckside, by W. Hawe. Small houses of 1885. Note the wider ground floor windows to let in more light where space was constricted.*

FIG. 245 (below left) *No. 20 New Walk. Detail of Eagle Patent Bedroom Grate (and Minton tiles).*

FIG. 246 (below right) *No. 20 New Walk. White marble chimneypiece. The extent to which the architect was responsible for the design of chimneypieces, etc., is problematic.*

FIG. 247 (top left)   *No. 110 Lairgate. Gothic porch c. 1825 perhaps based upon a design by P. Dekker. Among the few other contemporary Gothic houses is No. 11 Westwood Road and, of somewhat later date, Nos. 30-32 Flemingate.*

FIG. 248 (top right)   *St. Mary's School, Norwood, by J. W. & B. Atkinson of York, 1875.*

FIG. 249 (below left)   *Nos. 9-11 New Walk, built by Smith & Brodrick for themselves, c. 1878. The architects produced numerous plans for these houses, one of which (of 1878) is shown on the Back End Papers.*

FIG. 250 (below right)   *No. 3 New Walk, by Smith & Brodrick, 1876.*

FIG. 251 (top left) *Nos. 44-46 Westwood Road, by Smith & Brodrick, 1893. To appreciate the architects' change of style, c.f. fig.* 249. FIG. 252 (top right) *The County Hall, Cross Street, by Smith & Brodrick, 1890.* FIG. 253 (below left) *No. 43 North Bar Without (Oak House). Detail of oak ceiling by Smith & Brodrick, 1880.* FIG. 254 (below centre) *No. 43 North Bar Without (Oak House). Detail of main staircase carved by J. E. Elwell, 1880. By incorporating apparently ancient material (see the landing handrail), Elwell presumably intended to suggest that the balusters themselves were also rescued from earlier buildings. For a similar Elwell staircase, see No. 4 North Bar Without.* FIG. 255 (below right) *Nos. 3-5 Westwood Road by Smith & Brodrick, 1893. For plans see p. 104. It was unusual at this date for houses of this size to have fully equipped bathrooms.*

FIG. 256 (opposite) *Carved wood panel by James Holmes, 1865-1940. Holmes was one of many woodcarvers employed by J. E. Elwell. The low wages paid to woodcarvers prompted Holmes to set up on his own account — as a newsagent! The carving, which is out of one piece of wood, was done in the carver's leisure hours over a period of years. The original is slightly larger than the illustration. From time to time, Holmes also made and carved furniture, some of which, like the panel, remains in his descendants' possession.* FIGS. 257 (above right) and 258 (below left) *No. 43 North Bar Without (Oak House). Details of wood-work in the dining room. Note the Regency revival door-frame, an unexpected touch for 1880. The parquet floor is of a type more commonly found on the continent and the whole house may well reflect the influence of Elwell's tour of the Rhineland a few years earlier. A carved detail of the chimneypiece is shown in fig. 194.* FIG. 259 (below right) *No. 45 North Bar Without, by J. E. Elwell. A 'Queen Anne' revival of 1894. The mixture of Early and Late Georgian and Regency motifs shown here is characteristically Late Victorian.*

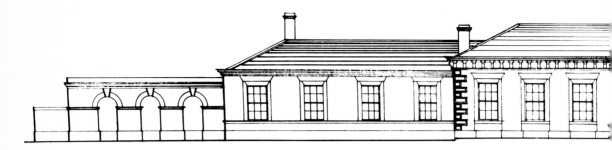

FIG. 260   *Front elevation of Beverley Railway Station before the remodelling of the principal entrance. Redraw. from a tracing in the British Rail Archives, York. The station was probably designed by the Railway Company's architec*

Victorian Architects and Builders

The following builders and architects are known (through advertisements in local newspapers and the plans deposited under the Public Health Act of 1848) to have worked in Beverley during the last half of the nineteenth century.

There is not space here to make a comprehensive list of buildings for which they were responsible though characteristic samples of their work are included in the list below.

With the exception of the Primitive Methodist Chapel in Wednesday Market all the buildings named are still extant.

The plans mentioned above also indicate the years of boom or slump in the local building industry: for example in 1872 only four projects were submitted but in 1879 as many as forty-one schemes were proposed. The average number of submissions however was between twenty and thirty, though an individual scheme might comprise anything from a simple alteration to existing premises, to a substantial block of new terrace houses.

JOHN BARNES *builder*
    39-49, 55-65 Beaver Road (formerly Boggle Lane)
    22-28 New Walk
    83-87 Norwood
    Others in Beckside, Holme Church Lane, Norwood.

ALFRED BEAUMONT *surveyor*
    Laboratory for Old Grammar School, Grayburn
      Lane
    1-5 John Street
    41-45 Wilbert Lane
    Alterations to 8 Ladygate and News Room, Cross
      Street.

WILLIAM BELL *architect of Hull*
    Railway Inspector's House, Mill Lane.

WILLIAM BOTTERILL *architect of Hull*
    Longcroft Hall (formerly St. Mary's Boys' School),
      Gallows Lane
    Alterations to 'Westwood', Westwood Hospital.

J. DALBY *builder of Hull*
    39-55 Wood Lane.

THOMAS DALTON *builder*
    34-42 Norwood Grove and others
    'Westwood View', Westwood Road
    48-50 Westwood Road
    23, 23a, 31-39 Woodlands
    25-29 Woodlands (with RICHARD FARRAH *joiner*).

WILLIAM HAWE *architect* 1822-97
    Fosters Yard, Beckside
    5-7 Eastgate
    119 Grovehill Road
    Stephenson's factory, Hull Bridge
    Minster Boys' School additions
    2-6, 8, 10, 20 New Walk
    Alterations to the Bar House, North Bar Within
    14, 16, 21 North Bar Within
    Alterations to 26, 28 North Bar Without
    1, 3 Norwood Far Grove
    Reading Room 'Ann Routh House', Toll Gavel
      (with J. R. FOLEY)
    2, 16-18, 60-65 Saturday Market, new shop 27
      Saturday Market
    Golden Ball Brewery, Walkergate
    Additions to Westwood Hospital (including
      gateway)
    Shop fronts at 11, 13 Wednesday Market
    Cemetery Lodges — St. Martin's Cemetery,
      Cartwright Lane and St. Mary's Cemetery,
      Molescroft.

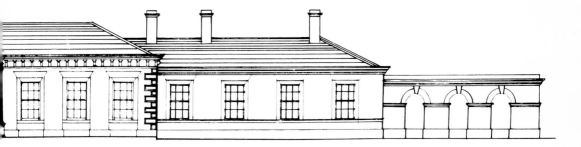

.T. Andrews. The original train shed was divided by a central row of columns. The present single span roof and scrolly ironwork ~ackets framing the entrance are Later Victorian alterations that also included the sacrifice of the Italian 'palazzo' entrance.

THOMAS MARSHALL *architect of Hull*
 20-22 St. Giles Croft.

WILLIAM MARSHALL *architect of Hull*
 52-54, Westwood Road
 House and stable, Willow Grove.

MORLEY and WOODHOUSE *architects of Bradford*
 Methodist Chapel, Toll Gavel.

SAMUEL MUSGRAVE *architect of Hull*
 Corn Exchange and Baths, Saturday Market.

EDWARD PAGE and GREGORY PAGE *surveyors*
 Designed and laid out Railway Street, Wilbert
  Grove and George Street
 Houses north side Railway Street.

GEO. PAPE *builder*
 Houses in Wilbert Grove
 Methodist Sunday School, Walkergate.

T. PEXTON
 10-12 George Street
 48-70 Wilbert Lane.

ANTHONY RICHARDSON *builder*
 1-6 Norwood Dale
 Stables, Willow Grove
 96-110 Norwood.

W. J. RICHARDSON *builder*
 4 North Bar Within
 6 Lairgate
 Westwood Hospital
 Restorations at St. Mary's.

THOMAS RIPPON *builder*
 2-10 St. Giles Croft
 30 Wilbert Grove.

FRANCIS SMITH *builder*
 13-25, 27-33 Cherry Tree Lane
 90, 97 (Common Lodging House) Flemingate
 151-155 Holme Church Lane
 56-64 Keldgate
 31 Ladgate (Common Lodging House)
 1-17 Spark Mill Terrace
 12-28 Westwood Road
 'The Meadows' and 'Westwood Close', Westwood
  Road
 28-34 Woodlands
 5-9 York Road.

R. G. SMITH and F. S. BRODRICK *architects of Hull*
 County Hall, Cross Street
 New school room, Minster Yard
 The Cottage Hospital, Morton Lane
 1-11 New Walk
 St. John of Beverley Church, North Bar Without
 'Oak House', 43 North Bar Without
 Alterations to Registrar's House, Register Square
 Almshouse, 20 Vicar Lane
 1, 3, 5, 44, 46 Westwood Road.

J. & R. STAMFORD *builders*
 24, 26, 28 Wilbert Grove.

WILLIAM THOMPSON *architect of Hull*
 19-21 New Walk.

MARMADUKE LOWSON WHITTON *builder* 1821-89
 (worked in conjunction with his brother JAMES
 WHITTON of Lincoln *architect*)
 2-20 Cherry Tree Lane
 40-52 Lairgate
 21-27 North Bar Without
 5, 7, 9, 11, 13 Westfield, Norfolk Street (converted
  from prison)
 The majority of houses in Willow Grove
 Park House, York Road
 3 York Road including stables
 10-25 York Road
 Many houses in Grovehill Road and Trinity Lane.

WRIGHT *architect of Hull* (pupil of CUTHBERT
 BRODRICK)
 Primitive Methodist Chapel, Wednesday Market.

FIGS. 261-4 *Show how from the 1870's onward the local style gradually gave place to one using readymade components manufactured elsewhere. Thus the arched doorheads and tiled panels are exactly as in Hull.* FIG. 261 (above left) *Nos. 118-20 Norwood. (A design probably derived from the porch by Thompson of Hull for Nos. 19-21 New Walk.)* FIG. 262 (above centre) *Panel of tiling at No. 175 Grovehill Road.* FIG. 263 (above right) *A pair of doorways at Nos. 155-7 Grovehill Road.* FIG. 264 (below) *Nos. 16-28 St. Giles Croft. Mostly developed by J. R. Blythe and by builders such as Thomas Rippon of Beverley and architects such as Thomas Marshall of Hull, during the 1870's.* FIG. 265 (opposite top left) *No. 61 Grovehill Road, built for W. H. Elwell c. 1877. An interesting example of Georgian survival.* FIG. 266 (opposite top right) *Detail of carved doorcase see fig. 265.* FIG. 267 (opposite right) *Alexandra Terrace, 25-29 Woodlands (formerly called Union Road because it led to the Workhouse). Built by Thomas Dalton and Richard Farrah, 1863. Note the eccentric placing of the oriel windows on the first floor.*

(*continued from page* 87).

laminated timber trusses must have made contemporary chapels seem very stodgy (*fig.* 269). The laminated truss was first used to roof great halls such as the Crystal Palace of 1851.

In the 1880's a new generation of speculative builders built much of the eastern part of Beverley, among them F. Smith, J. & R. Stamford and G. Pape. Thomas Dalton's work, some of it designed by Hawe, can be found off Norwood and in Woodlands (e.g. *fig.* 267). By the turn of the century, the Beverley builders had adopted a style similar to that of Hull (*figs.* 261-4), a process to be much intensified, and one perhaps best expressed in the concrete houses built upon the Menniel system just after the close of the Great War (*fig.* 270).

In the last half century, Beverley, like many other historic towns, has been subjected to many destructive pressures. At the time of writing several historic buildings are threatened with mutilation or destruction. Because less than a third of the buildings already 'listed' as of 'special architectural or historic interest' are described, it is to be hoped those unavoidably omitted are not dismissed as of secondary importance. Any selection has an element of the arbitrary: in our case we have simply sought out those buildings in whose construction or decoration often long-forgotten craftsmen have played a part.

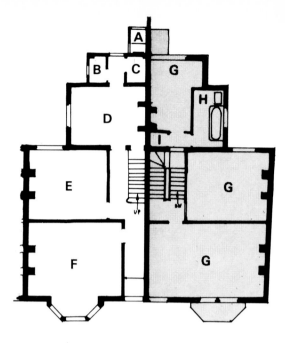

FIG. 268 (above) *Nos. 5-13 Westfield, Norfolk Street. Nos. 5-7 formerly housed the treadmill, Nos. 9-11 the turnkey's house and Nos. 11-13 were men's prison cells. Among the many graffitti still to be found cut in the brick-work are prisoners' calendars (used to mark off their sentences day by day), and inscriptions such as 'Oh! my poor leg' — a grim reminder of treadmills and leg-irons. The conversion was carried out by M. L. Whitton to designs of his brother James in 1880.* FIG. 269 (below) *Interior of the Salvation Army Citadel, Wilbert Lane by E. J. Sherwood of London, 1885. Internally, at least an interesting precursor of the functional architecture of the twentieth century.*

Nos. 3-5 Westwood Road (*see fig.* 255).

Ground floor plan (left) A - Earth Closet B - Pantry
C - Coal   D - Kitchen   E - Living Room   F - Sitting Room.

First floor plan (right)   G - Bedrooms   H - Bathroom
I - Linen.

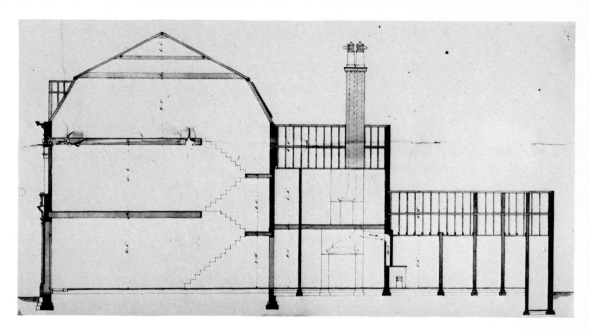

Section of 5-7 Eastgate, 1871 (above).

FIG. 270 (below)   *Nos. 215-23 Grovehill Road. This group of houses and its neighbours are a mixture of new and existing materials. They were designed by the former H.M. Office of Works at the end of the Great War. The layout of the nearby streets was the first in the town that was not constricted within the boundaries of former fields. The use of 'Georgian' sash barred windows in concrete houses is a striking example of Beverley's architectural conservatism. Among the architects who worked on the scheme was John Bilson (see p. 30).*

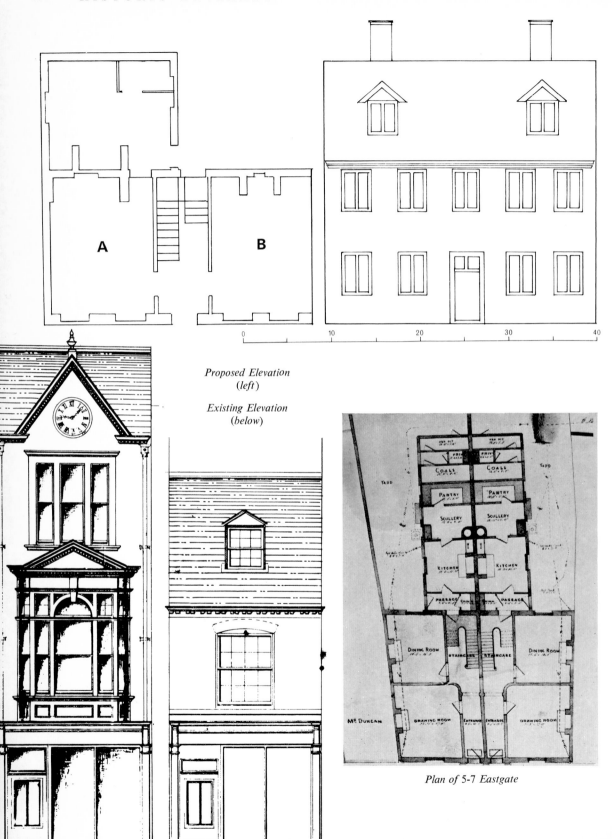

0   10   20   30   40

Proposed Elevation
(*left*)

Existing Elevation
(*below*)

Plan of 5-7 Eastgate

FIG. 273 (above) *Elevation of Nos. 69-77 Norwood, proposed to be built by Mr. John Parkinson, 1871.*

FIG. 271 (opposite top) *Contract drawing (redrawn) for Mr. Issott's house, Butcher Row, 1736. The front room (A) on the left was a kitchen. Note there is no end wall to the right of room (B), a once common practice, disguised by the use of wood panelling.*
FIG. 272 (opposite below left) *Drawing of proposed and existing new front elevations for No. 2 Saturday Market, 1885. The design was only partially carried out. PLAN (opposite below right) of 5-7 Eastgate by William Hawe, 1871. For elevation see fig. 240, for section see p. 105.*

Sources

The prinicipal general histories of Beverley are George Poulson's *Beverlac* and the Rev. George Oliver's *History and Antiquities of Beverley* both published in 1829. There are also a variety of nineteenth and twentieth century guides to the churches and to the town, such as J. Sheahan's *Handbook to Beverley* published by John Green, and C. Hiatt's *Beverley Minster*—published by G. Bell & Sons, London, 1899. There are also the entries in the various editions of *Kelly's Directories* and in Sir Nikolaus Pevsner's *Yorkshire; York and the East Riding* in the *Buildings of England* series, published in 1972; articles by K. A. MacMahon including *William Middleton* in the *Transactions of the Georgian Society of East Yorkshire* 1953-55, and an article by R. Whiteing in the latter journal of 1949-51 *Georgian Restorations of Beverley Minster.*

The chief documentary sources accessible to the public are the Borough Records (partly in the hands of the Corporation, partly deposited at the County Record Office), the series of private family archives, especially of families such as the Hothams who held property in the town (now in the County Record Office) and the 'memorials' that record land transfers throughout the East Riding from 1708 to the present day (housed in the East Riding Land Registry).

From these documents it is possible to glean the basis of an architectural history of the town. This information is supplemented by such well known sources as the series of parish registers, and by the Wills now kept at the Borthwick Institute at York. There is also an excellent series of books, drawings and engravings relating to Beverley in the York Minster Library. The quotation concerning the garden of St. Mary's Manor is taken from an article in *Country Life*, February 15th, 1973, by Dr. D. Linstrum and Dr. T. Friedman (*see page* 53).

It might be noted here that solicitors, when preparing a conveyance or a 'memorial' tended to repeat phrases such as 'lately rebuilt' even decades after the event and to repeat long outdated descriptions of locations, a practice that can lead to considerable confusion.

INDEX OF ARCHITECTS AND CRAFTSMEN

Page references in light type. Figure references in bold type.

See also list of Victorian Architects and Builders, pages 100-1.

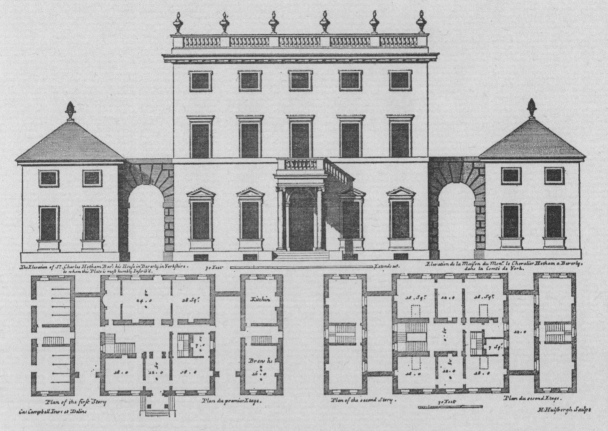

Plans and Elevation for Hotham House by Colen Campbell, 1716-21.

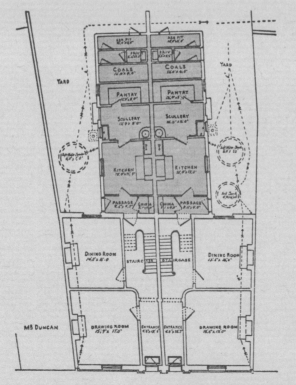

Plan of 5-7 Eastgate,
by William Hawe, 1871.